RAPE NEW YORK

T0266393

RAPE NEW YORK JANA LEO

THE
FEMINIST PRESS
AT THE CITY UNIVERSITY
OF NEW YORK
NEW YORK CITY

Published in 2011 by the Feminist Press
at the City University of New York
The Graduate Center
365 Fifth Avenue, Suite 5406
New York, NY 10016

feministpress.org

Originally published by Book Works, London, 2009 in the Semina series, No. 4.
Edited by Stewart Home and Gavin Everall.

First printing, February 2011

Cover design by Herb Thornby, thinkstudionyc.com
Text design by Drew Stevens

Library of Congress Cataloging-in-Publication Data

Leo, Jana, 1965–
    Rape New York / Jana Leo.
        p. cm.
    ISBN 978-1-55861-681-3
1. Rape—New York (State)—New York—Case studies. 2. Leo, Jana, 1965–
3. Rape victims—New York (State)—New York—Biography. I. Title.
    HV6565.N7L46 2011
    362.883092—dc22
    [B]

                                                                2010039974

PRINTED IN CANADA

FOR LESLIE BLUMBERG

CONTENTS

A NONVIOLENT RAPE

A Nonviolent Rape   3

How an Uneventful Day and Place Became Eventful   25

BEFORE AND AFTER A NONVIOLENT RAPE

How I Left Harlem   31

How I Had Ended Up in Harlem   36

How I Lost the Feeling of Being at Home   48

How and Why I Started a Lawsuit Against My Landlord   56

**THE CRIMINAL PROCEDURE AND THE
CIVIL LAWSUIT**

How the Assailant Was Caught   71

"Domestophobia" and PrisonLand   82

How the Assailant Was Convicted for Two Rapes   98

The Civil Lawsuit for Improper Security   111

DEFEATED BY NEW YORK

One of New York's "Ten Worst Landlords" Faces
Federal Charges   125

Defeated by New York, or, Why I Came to New York   130

Afterword   141

Acknowledgments   143

A NONVIOLENT RAPE

A NONVIOLENT RAPE

"YOU SCARED ME!"

I said it without screaming, as if he were playing a joke on me.

For a moment I thought he was a downstairs neighbor who sometimes smoked in the stairwell. Physically, he was similar and the light in the corridor was dim as my eyes hadn't had time to adjust from the harsh sunlight outside.

I couldn't believe there was a man with a gun in my doorway. My first response was denial: nothing bad would happen. My second reaction was to face the reality of the situation and to try and handle it as best I could.

"Do you have some money?"

"Yes, I think I have twenty dollars."

He entered my apartment. When I saw him cross the threshold between the corridor and my apartment, closing the door behind him, I realized that my everyday life was over. This was not a day like any other, this was the end, the last day of my life, or at least the last day of my present life.

"Go in."

He pushed the door to close it shut behind him, and then double-locked it.

His presence in my apartment was like losing blood, as if my space was being emptied of air. For an instant, as he moved along the hallway, I felt as if I was going to fall, that gravity could no longer support me. The space wasn't under my control because someone else had altered it. Entering my own apartment was entering another sphere, a world unknown to me, regulated by rules I had no knowledge of, a world in which I felt completely foreign. I would feel separated from the world to which I had, until then, belonged. He was a stranger, and his presence altered my life to such an extent that I too became a stranger, strange to myself, and strange to others. In this new world, I was conscious that at any moment my life could be taken from me: I had no control.

I put my shoulder bag down on a table in the living room and searched for my wallet. I found it and looked inside.

"I have thirty-one dollars."

I handed him thirty.

"Can I keep one? This is all the money I have."

I asked him if I could keep a dollar. The request, though I may not have been conscious of it at the time, was supposed to indicate that I had no more money in the house. It was also an attempt to retain some minimal control over my money and thus, over the situation. Asking to keep a dollar was the first sign of negotiation.

"OK. Sit down."

I sat on the red love seat that was my usual resting place when I was home. Sitting on this chair was a desperate effort to continue as if everything was normal. He sat down diagonally in front of me on a bed that I also used as a sofa. He held the gun with his hand resting on his leg, no longer pointing it at me.

"Can I have a cigarette?" he asked.

"Yes, sure."

Why was he asking me for things when he was inside my apartment without permission? He was polite, like someone visiting for the first time. But his politeness confused me.

He held a gun, but he was asking permission. Was he playing a game? If so, what game? I didn't understand the rules, and this disorientation made me nervous.

"Are you positive you don't have more money?"

"Yes. I am a student here. I study art downtown, and it is the end of the month."

"Do you live alone?"

"No, I live with my boyfriend."

"When is he coming back?"

"I do not know. I never know when he is coming. He comes back at a different time every day."

Why was he asking about my boyfriend? Did he want to know how much time he had alone with me? Was he going to wait until my boyfriend came home? My boyfriend had returned to Spain. He was not going to come back for three months. And my new roommate would not arrive until late that night, or possibly not until the following morning.

My mouth was dry. I needed to catch my breath. At the same time I needed to test my capacity for movement, to test my situation.

"Can I have a glass of water?" I asked.

"Yes."

I stood up and went into the kitchen.

"Do you want something to drink?"

I was surprised when I heard myself. I was addressing him as if he was a friend who'd come for a visit. But that was what I wanted to make him believe—that I was his friend— because he would not kill a friend. He would not kill such a friendly person. He would not murder a woman who asked him if he wanted something to drink. I went into the kitchen, hoping the window might be open. Sometimes, the guys in the front building smoked in the fire escape, but no one was there; it was winter.

He followed me in.

"Yes, give me some water too."

A big glass I had drunk water from that morning was still on the counter. I opened the kitchen cabinet on top of the dishwasher and looked for another glass. Glass or plastic? I took the plastic cup. I guessed, wrongly, that plastic was more conducive for a saliva trace.

We went back into the living room with the water. I sat down and drank slowly. We sat silently for several minutes.

The time without words was unbearable. I was being held hostage in my own house.

"Do you have a phone?"

"Yes."

The phone was next to the window, in front of him.

"Where?"

"Over there." I pointed to the phone.

"Do you have more money?"

"No."

What was the relationship between asking for the telephone and asking for money? Was he going to call someone? He picked up the phone to see if there was a connection. He dialed some numbers. I panicked. I feared he was calling his friends over. They were going to destroy my home and steal my things, my photographic equipment, my computer; then they were going to torture and kill me.

He made several calls, I counted ten numbers each call, but he didn't speak to anyone.

"Where is the bathroom?"

I stood and walked through the hallway to the bathroom. He followed me. I opened the bathroom door for him. He went in holding the gun in one hand and the phone in the other and stood there. He wants some privacy to talk, I thought, not knowing what to make of it. The bathroom door was in front of my apartment door. I wanted him to close the bathroom door so I could open the apartment door in front of it. But he didn't close the door. He just stood there with the telephone and the gun, looking at the apartment door.

What was he doing in the bathroom with the telephone? He didn't talk to anyone but stood looking at the receiver. I crossed the living room and went into the studio. The window led onto a fire escape, but the gate was locked and I couldn't open it.

The building's superintendent had installed the gate for us when we rented the place. I heard the man's steps and stopped trying the gate. On my way back to the living room I glanced at my open laptop. He looked at me as if to ask what I was doing. As he crossed the living room to put the wireless phone on its base, he stepped with his boots on a comforter.

"I am sorry."

His apology made me more anxious. He'd forced his way into my apartment with a gun, but he was apologizing for stepping on my comforter. Did that imply a disturbance in his personality? The first time someone comes into your home they are often excessively polite because they don't feel entirely comfortable and want to create an image of themselves as a nice person. Why was he so polite? What did it mean?

Was this the first time he had done something like this? Did his awkwardness come from having a gun, a weapon that can be used from afar and that gives a certain distance in perceiving the victim as real? Was he trying to make a good impression, as if we were on a first date? Was he trying to disorient me? I went along with his game because I wanted to survive. I was completely aware that it was a game, and I was able to distinguish the game from the reality of the situation.

"No problem, that's OK."

"Can I have another cigarette?"

Asking again? He hadn't asked me if he could enter my apartment. He was asking with a gun. What kind of psychopath was he? The weapon invalidated the option of saying no.

He was suggesting that I not only follow his orders, but also be cool about doing so. Was this a way of humiliating me?

"Sure, take another one."

My answer, like his question, maintained the impression that nothing out of the ordinary was happening. I was also playing a game, hoping to create empathy and thereby make violent behavior seem inappropriate. He rested the cigarette on the edge of my table. A game board resembling the plan and elevation of a building, which I'd made for my master's thesis, was on the table. It was constructed from metal, with magnetic figures that could be moved around like pawns in a game of chess.

"No, no, not there. Here, take the astray. This is a piece of art, my artwork, and I don't want it burned."

"OK."

Correcting him was a way of showing that I wasn't in a

state of panic. By making a small request I was also testing the limits of my influence or power over him.

"I'm sorry."

"That's OK."

He sat down again and remained silent for a few minutes.

There is something comforting about following a routine. Sequencing and planning create a feeling of control over one's actions, as if, in fact, one controls one's own life. Cook the potatoes and carrots, take the subway, go to the library. My daily sequence altered that day. My morning, starting at 9:30 a.m. with a doctor's appointment, getting a prescription and buying fresh food, had been wasted. I was no longer worried about the state of my health and other issues of everyday life but about having a life at all. I was forced to confront the possibility I might be killed.

"Are you sure you don't have more money?"

"Yes I am sure. Really. I get about a thousand a month for everything, you know. It's little money, and it's almost the end of the month."

I could see, like he could, my photographic camera on top of the tripod in the living room. It was odd that he didn't ask me for the camera; it was right in front of him. It was weird that he didn't look around the house for anything else of value. He didn't touch anything. He didn't even go into the studio or the bedroom.

"Do you go to college? Where?"

"Downtown. Educational Alliance."

The name came to my mind because I was entering in a competition for the renovation of that school.

"I start my class at five. I need to go."

"OK."

"What do you do?"

"I work in a restaurant."

"A restaurant, which one?"

"Adele."

"I don't know it, but I don't know any restaurants anyway."

"You don't know Adele? The one on Thirty-Fourth Street?"

"No, I don't."

A normal guy with a legitimate restaurant job who'd forced his way into my apartment with a gun? He was lying. But why a restaurant? Couldn't he imagine himself doing something else? Or was he following first date rules and imagined a restaurant worker suited a student? I thought of asking him why he was stealing money from me if he worked in a restaurant? Or was it better not to stretch the rules of his game, in case a harsher reality was revealed?

I thought of a mathematical progression, a sequence of three numbers that leads to a fourth. He had already committed a crime by entering my house. He'd committed another by pointing a gun at me, and a third by stealing my money. What would happen next? He was standing in front of me in the living room of my apartment bathed in sunlight. I looked at his face. I could identify him to the police. How was he going to prevent that? By killing me?

Statistics tumbled through my mind. My boyfriend, A, had been working on a project for his studio class about prisons and architecture. "One out of ten men in the US is or will be in prison. One out of four black men is or will be in prison." I felt nervous. What did he want? Did he enjoy playing with me? I was fully aware that I was the loser and he was the winner.

"Could you go? I need to do some things before I go to school. Could you please go?"

"I'm not going. I'll decide when I'm leaving. Don't tell me what to do."

He sounded angry and powerful: the voice of an enemy. He was showing how limited my power was. He was not going to go. Why not? What did he want? The questions in my head were overshadowed by panic: Why is he here? Why is he not going? Is he waiting for someone to come? What is he going to do to me? What is he waiting for? He is not looking at my things, he is just looking at me. He is just there sitting on the edge of the bed, looking at me. Is it me he wants?

At that moment I realized what he wanted was not related to my things, but to me.

I felt a deep fear surge through every part of my body, throwing me off balance. It was the fear of death, a fear so intense I didn't care about how I died, or what was expected of me before death. A pure fear without hope.

"Are you going to kill me?"

The words came directly from my gut.

I'd lost control of the situation. The words spilled from my mouth, alien, as if spoken by someone else. My fear wasn't so much a natural fear of death, but came from the absurd realization that a life could be threatened or terminated for another's entertainment. I saw the meaninglessness of existence. I have not been able to recover from that moment and don't expect to.

"No, I am not going to kill you."

"OK."

I relaxed a little, but I immediately entered into a new field of terror, envisaging physical torture. I was being held hostage in my own house, a place of safety, intimacy, and joy. I was trapped and knew that no one would be coming, that I could do nothing to escape. I could only play his game, not to win, but to lose less.

He stood up and moved toward the door, then sat down again.

"Do you live alone?"

"No, I told you. I live with my boyfriend."

"When is he coming home? Are you sure he is coming?"

"I do not know. He arrives at a different time every day. But yes, he will come."

My boyfriend wasn't coming home soon. I felt the man

with the gun somehow knew. Otherwise, why would he keep asking me the same question? Maybe he'd seen A leaving the building with his suitcase. Perhaps he'd noted there were only women's clothes and toiletries in the apartment.

"Are you sure you live with someone?"

"Yes. And you, where do you live?"

"Right across the street."

I imagined him watching me for the past ten days since I had returned from Spain, coming home alone. Perhaps he was one of the men that stood on the corner of 129th Street and St. Nicholas Terrace, standing in a circle, holding dollar bills; or one of the men who stood next to the grocery store across the street. Perhaps he had been watching me from somewhere even closer. Had he been watching me from inside the building? Was his presence in the building so familiar that I had not consciously registered him, but confused him with a downstairs neighbor? I'd heard noises on the roof that I'd reported to the super, thinking there were rats up there. Later, when I told the building superintendent what had happened, and described a husky, young, black man, five eight to five ten, one hundred eighty to two hundred pounds, in his early twenties, clean-cut with prominent features, brown eyes in a round, childish face, the super told me he'd seen a man of that description sleeping on the roof a couple of weeks earlier.

"I am going to the kitchen. Can I cook now?"

"No, not yet."

"No? It is getting late. I have to make my food and then I have to go to school."

"Not yet."

Yet. He had said it twice. It meant that something had to happen before I could get on with my everyday life. The yet told me he was about to do something.

"What do you want? Why are you here?"

"Lie down."

He was sitting on the bed looking at me, telling me to lie down. This was it.

"What do you mean, lie down?"

He held the gun up and pointed it at me. With a more violent tone, he repeated.

"Lie down."

He didn't want my camera, TV, or VCR. He wanted me. He didn't just want sex; he wanted to take me away from myself, to remove any sense of confidence from my person. The order meant that he was about to rape me. Afterward I thought about the meaning of making someone lie down, not only to force them into unwanted sex, but also to put them down, to diminish them, to take away their sense of self-respect and humiliate them.

I wanted to stay alive, and knew that I had to control myself. I knew that it meant making him feel that I was OK with being raped. I had to force myself to be collaborative.

"Do you want sex?"

I was terrified but in a way relieved; terrified at the idea of being coerced into sex, but relieved to know what he wanted, and that he might not kill me. After he'd raped me, he might leave. I hadn't thought about rape before this. Perhaps it was too horrible to think about. The gun was so present that death had been my only concern. I had been focused on how to stay alive. I was in love with my boyfriend and didn't pay attention to other men sexually. I wasn't used to seeing men as sexual predators. I'd been in a motorcycle accident and had just come from the doctor's. I had not thought about my body in a sexual way for some time. The man in my apartment was younger than I was and not bad looking. Perhaps I hadn't thought of rape because I was in my own home, in the room where I used to relax, sitting on my love seat. And this man with a gun was sitting on the bed where my boyfriend and I made love, on a comforter that had, for five years, covered our bodies.

"Yes."

"You know, we can talk about these things; you don't have to point the gun at me. I will do whatever you want me to do, just stop pointing the gun at me."

I remained on the red love seat, not moving.

"I have come from the doctor. I am sick. I don't think you want sex with me."

"I do."

"OK, OK. I will do it, don't worry. I will do it. You don't have to point at me with the gun. In fact, you don't have to have the gun at all when we're doing it."

He put the gun down.

"Let me get a condom, I have them right there."

I moved to the plastic drawer and grabbed a condom. He looked at it, as though he was not going to take it.

"I am sick. I have come from the doctor. I told you."

I rolled up my left jersey arm sleeve to show him the bandage from the blood test. I hoped he would associate my slight frame with the thinness of a person with AIDS.

I removed my brown boots and then my pants. I looked down. He had taken the condom and must have removed his two T-shirts in a single movement, because when I looked at him again he was barechested. The gun was on the table close to his right hand. He removed his gray wool hat revealing a do-rag that covered his hair. He must have been fairly certain I was not really expecting anyone. Otherwise, why would he have allowed the gun to leave his hand? I knew that he would follow my requests as long as they did not interfere with what he wanted.

"You are in good shape, do you work out? I am not in good shape, it is so embarrassing. Are you sure you want to do it?"

"You are in pretty good shape. Get undressed, right now."

I removed my jersey, my undershirt and my stockings. I was in my bra and underpants.

For the second time that day I was undressing: first it had been for the doctor, and now it was for a man with the gun.

It's just a question of thinking that nothing is happening, I told myself. Just act as if you're in the doctor's office and follow instructions. Don't think about what's happening to you. Just do what he's telling you and be nice and cooperative so it will be over quickly, like holding still for an X-ray. Just follow the instructions and make it easy.

"Is it OK like this?"

I didn't want to be naked in front of him and hoped that being in underwear would satisfy his first date fantasy.

"No, take it all off."

Still looking at the floor I removed my bra and my underpants and lay down across the shorter part of the bed, parallel to the pillow and to him. I wanted to make this as uncomfortable for him as I could. He'd pulled his pants down. His underwear was striped blue, black, and white. He'd put the condom on. I didn't look at him. I turned my head to the side. I opened my legs. He tried to put his penis in, but it wasn't easy. I was tense, my vagina was dry, and his penis was large. He was unable to enter me. It hurt.

"Have you had sex before?"

He couldn't understand why my vagina wasn't wet. He didn't understand that I could open my legs but not be wet if sex was not desirable to me. He didn't want to tell himself that I was following orders but my body was not.

"Yes."

"So, what happened?"

"Well you know it is weird, in this situation."

"I have the condom on right? So then there is no problem."

I didn't explain to him that two people need more than a condom to have sex. The condom was a protection but didn't make the sex consensual. I was being raped, even if it was a "nonviolent" rape. He'd entered my house with a gun, and now he was entering my body. That was not the way I did things. I made my own decisions regarding sex: chose when, how, and with whom. I had the right to refuse without argument or threat. But principles do not apply under the threat of death. If I had to choose between "my virtue" or my life, there was no doubt. I chose to assume a loss in order to minimize loss. Death offers no way back. I understood this mentally, but my body refused to accept it.

He held me by the waist and licked my right breast. I tried to relax in order to make things easier and less painful. His penis wouldn't go in so he pushed harder, helping himself with his hand to penetrate my body. It hurt. It had never hurt that much before. I felt my flesh was about to break.

I stared at the ceiling taking in absurd details. I noticed that the paint wasn't completely flat but had a granular texture and formed a vague pattern. I focused on the grainy irregularity and random pattern, a landscape formed by small dots of dusty white covering a perfect white. I tried to imagine the original surface underneath disturbed by the granulated paint. It was erased, covered by sloppy tiny patches of Wite-Out. It was so sad to see those defective dots with their undefined shapes, dots that I couldn't reach with my hands, with my body forced against a stranger. I should not cry. I couldn't let myself go in any way. I had to put all my energy into staying alive.

"Can I kiss you?"

I stared at him. This guy is crazy. He enters my house with a gun, enters my body without permission. Now he asks if he can kiss me. What is the point of asking if he can kiss me when he is taking me by force? He acts as if he's having sex with a girl for the first time. Is this the fantasy? That he is my boyfriend, or that we're having a first date and a first kiss? Maybe he won't kill me if I'm the girl of his fantasies: his girlfriend or his first date. He'll, most likely, not kill me if I help him live his fantasy instead of stopping it. I have to remain passive, so that I am not who I really am, but a figment of his imagination.

He kicked off the pants and underwear that had been pulled down to his ankles.

"Yes."

Sometimes yes means no. I forced myself to let him kiss me. He kissed me smoothly on the lips, while I remained flat, lifeless, like a doll. It looked like he wasn't getting excited enough, probably because I didn't move or do anything.

"Do you like it?"

"It is not too bad."

If I faked liking it, he might be faster. But he might also

think that I shouldn't enjoy it because he was raping me, and if I showed too much pleasure I deserved to be killed. Maybe that wasn't his mindset at all, but who was to know? I didn't. All I knew was that I couldn't take the risk. I tried to be as neutral as possible and didn't force the situation to avoid it becoming something even worse than it already was.

He touched my anus with his fingers and started to pull out his penis from my vagina to put it in my anus.

"No, no, please, I am sick. No, no, please. I am sick. No, no, please, it will hurt so much."

I'd experienced pain in my intestines for the past three days and had cramps. Though he was already raping me I pleaded as much as I dared knowing that some negotiation was possible. He pushed his penis back into my vagina and pulled my body to his. He began to move faster. He continued like that for some time. I do not know for how long, maybe five minutes, maybe seven or ten. The last two minutes, he increased the rhythm and kept moving faster until he stopped. I guess he ejaculated. He remained still for a minute on top of me and then he pulled out.

"I had some fun," he said, with a smiling, happy face.

I saw the condom in his hands; he was making a knot in it.

We both started dressing. I dressed quickly, pushed by the fear of what might happen next.

"Do you always meet women like that? Why do you meet women like that, you know, with a gun? I am sure there are a lot of women who want to meet you without the need of the gun."

"They don't. They don't want to do it. I am so shy."

I had to try to persuade him to go and not come back. He had to think that I didn't have anything against him, but I could not do it again.

"I have a boyfriend. We love each other. We really do and we made this commitment of not going with anybody else. I am sure you will find someone, but please don't come back; otherwise my boyfriend may find out, and it is going to be really bad for all of us."

I was trying to feed his fantasy; we were having an affair, but it was impossible to keep it going. I was in love. There was nothing wrong with him.

He had put on his T-shirts, shoes, and pants. He took the gun from the table and put it in his pocket. He opened the window to throw the condom away.

"No, somebody may see it. Give it to me."

I took it from his hand and went to the kitchen to put it in the trash. I wanted to keep it as a trace, as proof of what he'd done. Did he know what I was doing?

"Your boyfriend will find it there."

"OK yes, how stupid! Yes, you are right."

He took it from the trash and put it in the toilet.

"No, no it never works. It will float."

He flushed the toilet. It disappeared.

He came back to the living room and started looking again at my black bag on top of the table.

"What do you want? I told you I don't have any more money."

He took my wallet out of the bag and looked at everything inside it. My American Express credit card, my faculty ID from Cooper. I was alarmed. He would discover I was lying, that I was not a student. But he didn't seem to care. Was he aware that just as he was playing out a fantasy, I was lying to fit the person in that fantasy?

"Do you have a driver's license?"

"Yes, it is there."

He picked up one of the ID's in my wallet and started reading it: Recreational Center. He was going to keep it.

"That is the ID to the swimming pool, the one close to here. The swimming pool is great."

"Where it is?"

"Just across the park on 135th Street."

"Uhm . . . Yeah."

"Do you go there?"

"Yes."

He took my ID and held it.

"What are you doing? Why do you want my ID? First, you took my money and now you're taking my pool ID, so I can't even go swimming. Why do you want it?"

"In case you go to the police."

"Why should I go to the police? You have a gun, right? You will kill me if I go to the police."

"I will kill you."

I extended my right hand asking for his.

"Let's make a deal, I am not going to the police and you will not come back, OK?"

He handed my ID back and gave me his hand.

"I will not go, why should I go? Everything is OK, just don't come back, OK? My name is Jana, what's yours?"

"Bennie. My name is Bennie."

He walked ahead of me down the hall, and I opened the door for him. He left without looking back.

HOW AN UNEVENTFUL
DAY AND PLACE
BECAME EVENTFUL

AFTER WAKING UP TIRED for several days, I decided to go to the doctor. My boyfriend A recommended one he had used. My body ached, especially my feet and hands. I had reasons to be physically exhausted. I'd finished my thesis that summer, then packed all of the things we had accumulated during our three-year stay at Princeton. A motorcycle accident had left me with abrasions on my abdomen and a broken clavicle. I'd just completed a draining search for an affordable apartment while teaching my first semester at Cooper Union and simultaneously flying back and forth to Madrid to secure a visa. A, whom I had lived with for a number of years, needed to return to Spain, which meant I needed a roommate to cover the rent. Despite these setbacks, the major effort was over. I was shattered, but looking forward to starting a new life.

When the nurse at the doctor's office asked me what was wrong, I told her I was suffering from exhaustion. She told me that she, too, was feeling a lack of energy, which I could see was true from the slow, lethargic way she moved. "Did you have a blood test?" I asked, while she filled vials with my blood. "No," she replied. "You should," I said, which made her smile. I had to wait a long time to see the doctor. I had been to his office once before with A and he made us wait then too, at least an hour and a half in the office.

My plan for the day had been to buy groceries, collect a prescription, eat, rest, and then work. I got out at 125th Street. The trip was fast; one stop to Fifty-Ninth Street and then an express to 125th. I walked to the Duane Reade Pharmacy on 125th, then to C-Town, the supermarket on the corner of 125th and Broadway. I bought a big bag of oranges, three grapefruits, orange-papaya juice, a bottle of milk, a container of yogurt, some potatoes, carrots, and bread. The four plastic bags, two in each hand, were difficult for me to carry. Only six months had passed since my motorcycle accident and just three since the metal pins had been taken out of my clavicle. As I carried the groceries, I practiced the breathing and diaphragm exercises that A had given me to take stress off my lower back. He was good at giving medical advice, but not at helping me pack, I thought.

I walked up Amsterdam Avenue past the hairdresser, the liquor store, the swimming pool closed for the winter, and the bus station on the other side of the street. I felt tired and walked slowly, observing the neighborhood. I went up the hill at 129th Street with its strange half-industrial, half-residential landscape, to Convent Avenue. Close to home, I crossed the street. Good buildings, but poorly maintained, I thought, as I turned in at 408 West 129th Street, where I lived.

I went up the front steps and put down my bags so I could get my keys. The lock was broken and the door was open. I would have to write another complaint. I was really tired of writing these letters, but the landlord ignored phone calls. I went up, happy to be nearly home with healthy food for the week. I smiled at one of my neighbors. She was a friendly older woman in her sixties, who always dressed with care. She reminded me of L, a neighbor in Madrid, whom I'd passed on the stairs for ten years. L had died the previous summer. I often thought about her and all those women who wear skirts and hose, even in winter, to buy a pound of sugar. Too cold for me. I was dressed in a dark green turtleneck sweater, orange jacket, and brown mountain hat.

I opened the door of my apartment with my shopping bags hanging from my arms and took them into the kitchen. I put them down and walked back toward the entrance door while removing my hat and my bag. The apartment was stiflingly hot, in stark contrast to the months I had endured with no heat at all. When I went to close the front door, a man with a gun was standing in the doorway.

BEFORE AND AFTER A NONVIOLENT RAPE

HOW I LEFT HARLEM

AS SOON AS THE RAPIST turned his back and stepped out of my apartment, I slammed the door shut, not caring where he went, then went into the living room and picked up the telephone. The red power light was on, but there was no tone. After pressing all the buttons, I looked inside the phone where the batteries were housed and saw that a wire had been disconnected. I kept an extra phone in case of power cuts, which I plugged in. I sat on the gray garden chair A had brought down from Princeton. I dialed his number.

"Something happened. Sit down."

My boyfriend was adamant that I should go to the police, but he was in Spain and hadn't been threatened with a gun. Still, I trusted his advice. I called the landlord's office and told his agent, M, that I had been assaulted. I asked her to fix the downstairs lock right away so the rapist couldn't enter easily if he returned. She told me she would have the lock fixed. Then I looked through the yellow pages and called the sex crimes report line. They transferred me to the Twenty-sixth Police Precinct. I spoke with a woman, Sergeant G. She wanted to send a police car, but I asked her not to do this. I imagined the rapist watching, seeing the police car, and shooting me. I was afraid of walking to the police station alone, but I was even more fearful of the rapist seeing the police come into my building.

My camera on the tripod in the middle of the living room was loaded with film. I took pictures of the traces the intruder had left in my apartment: the ashtray with the two cigarette butts, the white plastic cup from which he drank water, and the white comforter on the bed with wrinkles revealing the shapes of bodies. After putting on gloves, I put the cup and ashtray in separate plastic bags. I walked to the Thirty-Second Precinct at 250 West 135th Street between Seventh and Eighth Avenues. I knew the location as it was on the way to the recreational center where I swam. I hesitated at the door, then I went to the front desk. The process started.

After relating what happened to a male officer, I was transferred to another room where I was asked the same questions by a second male officer. Another two then took me to St. Luke's Emergency Department, and on the way, the female officer, sitting in the passenger seat, questioned me again as she filled in a report. After waiting more than an hour at St. Luke's, I was taken to an examination room. I got undressed for the third time that day. My jeans, sweater, underwear, socks, and bra were collected, leaving me with just my jacket and boots. I wore them along with a hospital gown that a nurse had given me.

While I was in the previous room waiting to be examined, a nonuniformed man introduced himself as Detective M from Manhattan Special Victims Squad. He questioned me again and requested that I tell my new roommate not to go to the apartment. He said he needed to take evidence, and to photograph the crime scene before anybody could enter. I didn't want any more strangers in my apartment but gave him my keys. I asked him to bring me some clothes when he returned. The doctors ran a series of tests, gathering evidence from my body. They took pictures of my vagina, of both the outside and the inside.

After a couple of hours, D, my boyfriend's brother, appeared at the door.

"How did you find out?"

"I called my brother to tell him that I was fired from my job. He told me what happened to you and asked me to go to your apartment because he was worried. Nobody was there. I saw a police car and asked them if they were there for any special reason, and I gave them your name. The police told me you were here."

He started crying.

"Why are you crying?"

"I lost my job."

It was dark when I got out of the hospital. Police officers drove D and me to my apartment. I got out of the police car in front of my building, wearing nothing but boots, a pair of pants, and the hospital gown under my jacket. Being home felt threatening. I asked the policemen to check the roof, which they did reluctantly, assuring me no one was there. My apartment was covered with gray fingerprinting dust. Later that night, officers took me to the Police Archive on Amsterdam Avenue and I looked at pictures of criminals to see if any matched the assailant. In the days that followed I spent more time in the archive looking at pictures. In a large open-plan room filled with empty office desks in front of two holding cells at the 125th Street Precinct, I watched surveillance videos. Except for an officer who sat at the far end of the office, I was alone. The videos showed men loitering in lifts, their faces hidden in the camera's blind spot. One of the videos captured what looked like a man actually raping a woman. I didn't see my assailant, and couldn't bring myself to return to the precinct to look at more videos. Going back to my apartment, I found the building's locks were still not working, and the roof doors were wide open. I was terrified I would see my attacker again.

ON SUPER BOWL SUNDAY, three days after the attack, P, a close friend and classmate from Princeton, came to see me. When I told him in detail what had happened, he urged me to move out immediately. I also spoke with C, a friend of mine from Spain, who was living in New York. She called me later that morning.

"He is going to get excited watching the Super Bowl. You have to move this Sunday before the game ends. If you wait one more day, it may be too late."

"You are delirious."

C told me to pack. She came over with her husband and a friend of his while the game was still on. We called a car. My boyfriend arranged that I temporarily move with a few belongings to his brother's apartment on the Upper West Side.

I lived there for two months and then moved in with my friend L for another couple of months. During this time, I continued to hold on to the apartment in Harlem, not wanting to give up my past.

HOW I HAD ENDED UP IN HARLEM

ON MY FIRST NIGHT in Princeton, I cried nonstop. The humid atmosphere made it feel like a suburban rainforest, too green and too clean for me. I had arrived late in the evening at the end of August 1997 with my boyfriend A, and a yellow suitcase, to live out his dream rather than my own. During my three long years in Princeton, I learned how to drive and even how to enjoy the green of the American lawn, but the suburbs didn't suit me. I wrote a paper, "Domestophobia: An Approach to the Deconstruction of the Concept of the Domestic as a Pleasurable Space in the US in the 1970s," and I graduated in May 2000. What I had learned about architecture was that buildings are game boards with people as pawns moving across the boards. For my master's thesis I made a building game board with magnetic figures, which I placed on a metal surface on top of a coffee table.

Before leaving Princeton, I temporarily stored my coffee table and other things at P's, and parked the 1972 Mercedes 240 in the parking lot in front of my old house in Butler graduate housing, and left for New York. I had a few days to look for an apartment, and a job before going to Spain for the summer. B, a classmate, took me to Williamsburg, Brooklyn. Only the Domino Sugar factory held some appeal for me. Another classmate suggested I look for a place north of Columbia University. He told me to start with apartment postings at bus stops. There were none at 116th Street. I took the 1 train to 145th Street and Broadway. Around 143rd Street on Broadway I saw a note in a barbershop: *Se rentan cuartos.* I talked to the woman in charge to see if she knew anything about apartments for rent in the area. She replied, "*Vete a ver a Wilfredo*," and wrote an address on a piece of paper.

I walked to the building, south on Broadway and left onto 129th Street. When I buzzed the doorbell no one answered. I sat on the stairs to the entrance of the building to rest and wait. It was early in the afternoon and there were no passersby. Some neighbors sat outside in chairs as if the sidewalks were an extension of their living rooms.

A man in a sleeveless T-shirt came up the stairs. I asked him if he knew the super. He told me he was the super. He had a friendly face. I asked if there were any apartments available. He said he was on his way to do some construction work in a vacant apartment, but it was not ready to rent. I asked him to show me the place. He didn't reply, but let me follow him in. On the way up the stairs we passed an elderly couple whom I thought would make nice neighbors.

The super showed me a one-bedroom apartment. The

kitchen was at the entrance and the living room looked south toward the Empire State Building. The apartment was filthy. There was graffiti on the walls, thick dirt on the floor, and a sofa with its upholstery ripped lay upside down. There were clean round holes in the walls in two places and they looked like bullet holes. I found it hard to believe what I saw. It looked like a set from a detective show on TV. The super said several apartments would be renovated by the fall, either in this building or in the one adjacent. I wrote down his phone number.

Ready to take my first holiday in three years, I left to join A in Spain. A few days before a scheduled trip to the Greek islands, I had a motorcycle accident. The skin of my abdomen was severely lacerated and my clavicle broken. I spent most of July in Madrid looking at the ceiling from the bed in A's apartment. By the time my skin had healed, and the bones knitted, the summer was gone. I left for New York during the last week of August, after the pins had been removed from my shoulder. A had left earlier to find a place for us to live.

When I arrived in New York, A was still looking for apartments and staying at his brother's place where I joined him. In the mornings we looked for a place to live, and in the afternoons we taught architecture. Rehabilitation exercises for my left shoulder ended the days.

"Come on, you can do it, a little bit more."

I would lie down on the floor, and A would rotate my arm a little more every day, stopping only when the pain brought tears to my eyes.

He'd contacted the super of the building on West 129th Street, seen the apartment, and liked the area, particularly its industrial look, accentuated by the elevated train on 125th Street. The neighborhood was a friendly mix of Hispanic and African Americans who took little notice of him. The building was affordable and close to Avery Library, the architecture library with the Mies van der Rohe archive at Columbia University.

With only a small budget we also looked at apartments in Greenpoint, a Polish neighborhood, recently populated by easygoing young people who were being pushed further into Brooklyn by the high rents in neighborhoods close to the bridges. Williamsburg and later Greenpoint were areas preferred by Spaniards in New York. The buildings emulated American suburbia, but they were also bathed in nostalgia for another place: a Europe that no longer exists. Harlem, on the other hand, felt part of New York City. The buildings there were well constructed and residential; and one could see the traces of different generations, nationalities, and ethnicities. African Americans, displaced from Greenwich Village, had arrived in Harlem, replacing the Dutch, and later the Jewish communities who'd lived there previously. For most of the twentieth century Harlem had been a home for black culture. Hit hard by depression, unemployment, and crime, Harlem showed its economic decline in its abandoned buildings and tired faces, but it also showed signs of its vibrant potential. Unlike Greenpoint, which resembled a work camp for immigrants, Harlem still revealed the power it had to produce culture from displacement.

WHILE A LIKED the area and the apartment on West 129th Street, he was concerned about moving to Harlem. For him the name Harlem brought to mind racial and economic segregation and crime. We didn't know whether the paths to crime and prison—family breakdown, poor education, unemployment, and drug dealing—myths associated with black Americans, had any basis in reality. Nor, if the myth of the American dream countered this stereotype in any way. In addition, A was concerned for my safety.

"With that curly blond hair you have, all the *negrillos* are going to want you."

I thought he was scared, and because I wasn't, I pushed aside his objections to settling in Harlem.

"I have kinky hair, I am a *negra-blanca*. They will notice."

We paid a deposit on one of the apartments that was being renovated. A rented *Robocop*. In the movie, real estate developers, in conjunction with the government, bring crime into downtown Chicago, making the area unlivable. When the buildings are abandoned, they buy them up, and by emptying buildings in this fashion, they circumvent housing regulations.

Robocop was a fictional version of what was happening in Harlem. Empty buildings were being torn down, becoming the vacant lots that one day would house condos. I was worried about being resented as representatives of the gentrification of the area that was displacing its black community. A and I stood out because we were white. But we were not the SUV drivers from New Jersey, who one sees now, seven years later, parked at 145th Street and Amsterdam in front of "condos for sale" signs. While we were privileged, we were economically impoverished. But we were afraid of how we might be perceived in Harlem.

INTRODUCING CRIME into an area is part of a crude development strategy. The more sophisticated and perverse approach is to simultaneously clamp down on street crime while forcing it into specific buildings targeted for speculation. Containing crime in specific buildings reduces their value so developers can purchase them inexpensively. Not only were developers able to buy property on the cheap, the scam also made short-term, low-income rentals much more profitable than high-income rentals. Contained within targeted buildings, crime was facilitated by a lack of security in the common areas, encouraging a rapid turnover of tenants. Agents kept the security deposit, increased the rent, and charged illegal brokers' fees, thus quickly realizing a profit from the quick turnover of tenants. If a third of the tenants in a thirty-apartment building moved annually, income doubled, yielding up to an extra one hundred thousand dollars. Eventually the building would fall completely vacant, and was no longer subject to rent stabilization laws. It would then be demolished or converted into luxury housing. When I moved to Harlem I wasn't aware of how the mechanics of these operations worked in detail, nor how they related to our new apartment and our lives.

We moved in October 2000. We spent the autumn sorting out the apartment as our home and office. A assembled tables and bookshelves, installed lighting, and hung photos. My strength often failed me when we moved furniture as I had not completely recovered from my motorcycle accident. I did the painting, and organized the cabinets. The weather was still warm and A began to go to a basketball court, joining the young men playing in the park on the corner of 129th Street and St. Nicholas Terrace. Outside the basketball court, a group of men sat on a bench for hours at a time. People approached them for short interactions and left. Often, I would walk to the top of the park and back down to pick A up. Sometimes I just watched him play. We also combined our time doing research at the Avery Library with part-time teaching jobs. I taught architecture at Cooper Union, assisting one of my former professors at Princeton. A held the post of visiting professor at Pratt, teaching an architecture course called PrisonLand. Recent findings from the US Bureau of Justice Statistics, which indicated that one out of twenty Americans would serve time in prison during their lifetime, functioned as the starting point for his course.

A map by Columbia University's Spatial Information Design Lab and the Justice Mapping Center shows that the New York prison population largely comes from a few neighborhoods such as Brownsville and Harlem. The map cross-references the annual cost and population of prisoners with the place where they lived before they were incarcerated, evaluating how much blocks in a certain area cost the government. The study found that a disproportionate number of inmates come from a limited number of neighborhoods, and also from specific blocks in these districts. The cost of incarceration has led these blocks to become known as "Million Dollar Blocks."

The unusual parameters and the precise focus of the study shows the concentration of crime within specific blocks in certain neighborhoods. But the restricted approach of the study, which looks at the cost relationship between the prison population and original residence in isolation, fails to address the wider implications. No link is made between the neighborhoods and blocks that disproportionately supply the prison population, and the location of the recent explosion in property development. While the study draws costs conclusions, it fails to develop the analysis and consider how the concentration of crime in certain blocks affects the profitability when those blocks are targeted for development. The study also leaves the implication of the "Million Dollar Block" unchallenged; that the cost of incarceration and crime is borne by the US government, and thus fails to consider the costs for the victims of crime, and the financial implications for the area's nonincarcerated residents.

Applying the *Robocop* analogy to the "Million Dollar Block" phenomenon, an elaborate operation unfolds, like a plot for a movie. The "Million Dollar Blocks" become a source of income for governmental agents in a world that follows the *Robocop* principle of corruption: introduce crime into an area to decrease real estate value, buy up land when the prices are down and then develop the neighborhood. Taxpayers bear the cost of crime, while the revenue created by real estate speculation remains in the hands of corrupt officials, slum landlords, and developers—with a payoff tax benefit going to city and state government. In a *Robocop* world, the million-dollar cost of a high-crime block paid by taxpayers yields a much greater revenue for speculators and government. The money spent on crime and incarceration is considered an initial investment for much greater return and increase in tax revenue from upscale development. Each "Million Dollar Block" is a gold brick radiating profit.

A AND I SHARED our research and compared it with the reality that surrounded us. The stately architecture of Harlem was at odds with what was going on inside it. The buildings were shells, and fortresses. The one we lived in didn't offer basic services, like hot water or an uninterrupted supply of electricity. It was badly maintained and poorly secured.

"You don't like it, move out."

That was the landlord's answer to our complaints. We didn't know what to do, but moving out wasn't a realistic option. We'd paid three months rent in advance when we signed the lease, and put a lot of work into making the apartment our home, and now lacked the funds to pay another deposit for a better apartment. At that time we didn't know about our rights as tenants or that a government agency, the Department of Housing Preservation and Development, enforces minimum conditions. We saw the lack of security but hoped that it wouldn't affect us, thinking that criminals would prefer to target wealthier locations.

A spent a great deal of time in the Mies van der Rohe Archive looking for the column that was erased from the architect's drawings for his *House for a Bachelor*. I was researching games, urban space, and architecture at the Avery Library, and at Columbia. Conscious of my everyday experience of the city as a continual crossing of borders, I developed a narrative of urban space as a game board: (one) pass people sitting aligned on the steps of Low Memorial Library overlooking the quad; (two) exit the gate of Columbia University at Broadway; (three) walk down the hill; (four) pass the buildings perfectly aligned to the curb; (five) feel a sense of disorientation when the projects recede from the curb not facing the street; (six) see the elevated train emerging from underground at 121st, the station marking the limit of 125th Street; (seven) cross the street; (eight) take the alley running past the police station, the parking lot and the church; (nine) smell the live chickens at the slaughterhouse and the exhaust from the bus depot; (ten) turn uphill toward St. Nicholas Terrace; (eleven) encounter the people standing on the corners like signs; (twelve) watch the people crowding onto the benches in front of the basketball court. Unlike most academics, I made my life and surroundings the subject of my research. I wasn't content to camouflage myself in the bubble of academia at Columbia University. A and I often laughed at the contrast between the university and Harlem, so close yet so removed from each other. Coming from another bubble, Princeton's School of Architecture, we knew that we didn't belong to either of these worlds. Living in Harlem we crossed invisible borders every day.

We took our personal experience of housing conditions in Harlem, and our neighborhood, and extrapolated theories on real estate, crime, and the architect's mission in the city.

We talked about architects proselytizing the benefits of new buildings, and developers making money from the decay and regeneration of neighborhoods. We compared the architect to the conflicted figure of the good policeman fighting crime in *Robocop*. A said that since Le Corbusier, the architect, had become a heroic figure, architects were the ones in charge of maintaining order in society. I felt that architects and developers enjoyed a corrupt symbiotic relationship. Rather than having a strong commitment to changing housing conditions, architects colluded with the exploitation of developers, neglecting basic human needs. Some days the problems with the hot water and security overwhelmed us, and we went to sleep early, not wanting to talk about anything.

By the end of November, A learned that this was his last chance to complete a credit toward his PhD, and started thinking of going to Spain for a semester. We'd lived together for many years and I was upset at the prospect of not having him around. Apart from losing his love, support, and friendship, practically it meant that I'd have to find a roommate since I could not cover the rent of our apartment alone. He pushed the date ahead as far as he could, and left on New Year's Eve 2000.

The discussions A and I had about architecture, prisons, and property development ended with his departure. But the questions we had raised together about the precise operations of crime and speculation were soon raised again by my assault. The lack of security in our building revealed another sinister game, which I'd not considered during my research into borders and boundaries. I discovered that the reason people moved through the buildings freely was to move without being seen. Buildings provided hidden routes, used by criminals to avoid detection. It was possible to enter a unsecured buildings from the street, go up the stairs, access the roof, and cross from one roof to another building, go back down to the street, without exposing one's movement. In 2005, a detective hired by my lawyer discovered that my building was known to the NYPD as a common location of crimes, and a frequently used residence of criminals.

HOW I LOST THE FEELING OF BEING AT HOME

AS I WAS ON MY WAY to pick up mail from my old apartment a couple of weeks after the rape, I thought I saw my assailant in the corner grocery store. Detective M told me this was normal, and that though I might be certain I was seeing him in many places, I would be wrong. On a Saturday afternoon a few weeks later, as I went upstairs to see the people who were staying in my apartment, I encountered him on the second-floor landing.

"Hi," he said.

"Hi," I replied.

Fear cut through me. I continued up to the fourth floor, then down again. I ran to a pay phone and called the police. This time, I had no doubt it was him. I met the police at the phone booth, got in the car, and drove around the street searching for my assailant. The day he raped me was in the middle of winter, but he wore no jacket, and he was not wearing one today. Only someone who lived nearby would travel without a coat. From the back of the police car I gazed at every young, black man without a jacket in the neighborhood. We covered the area, passing every street at least three times, the eyes of passersby looking at me inside the car. I tried to look while hiding in the back of the car. After a couple hours of unsuccessful searching, the policemen asked me where he could take me, and drove me back to the Avery Library at Columbia University.

WITHIN WEEKS the direction of my thesis had altered as I tried to answer the crucial questions in my own life. Did my assailant live in my area? Would he return? As I couldn't answer these personal questions, they were translated into others that refocused the thesis. What is the operational radius of a rapist? Is a rapist likely to return to rape? Is there a pattern of criminal behavior, where rape is followed by murder? Where does rape happen and where doesn't it happen?

As I looked at the statistics, it became clear how the myths associated with rape and the home were intertwined. The idea that rape happens at night, in dark alleys, in alien locations, is false. It is a myth that nourishes the image of the house as a safe place, offering comfort and suppressing the threat of rape from the mind. This mythology serves a masculine interest, with its lust for the free availability of women within the sanctuary of their home.

After being held hostage in my apartment and raped, I didn't feel at home anywhere or with anybody. I didn't feel safe at home or anywhere. I found myself disappearing into nonplaces: computer rooms, libraries and coffee shops, or friends' studios, or darkrooms.

The idea that rape is a rare event, occurring beyond familiar places, dissociated from the ordinariness of the everyday, is an illusion. In reality rape is not associated with risk, adventure, or the unknown; 94 percent of rapes and sexual assaults occur within fifty miles of the victim's home. It frequently occurs in the home, and is often committed by those with whom the victim feels comfortable. Police call such offenders "known doers." Men who live in the victim's house, relatives, or men with whom the victim has social contact constitute 75 percent of rapists. One in four female rape victims is raped in or around her own residence.

I reread my Princeton paper on "Domestophobia." In the United States, rape is a common occurrence; it happens to one in six women. It is an extraordinary event for the victim, but an ordinary action: not only in the sense that it happens so frequently, but because it usually happens during familiar routines, and in the course of everyday actions. Opening the door when coming home from the grocery store, putting the rubbish in the basement. Ordinary actions performed automatically or in a state of distraction in close proximity to the victim's home or workplace.

Intruders (25 percent of rapists) take advantage of fragile moments, such as opening the front door of a building, or entering an apartment. Assault is more likely to happen in transitory spaces such as entryways, staircases, elevators, basements, roofs, lobbies, corridors, and entrance halls. Rape occurs most often in places where a certain intimacy is possible. As defined in the "Take-Home Instructions for the Patient" I got at the St. Luke's Emergency Department, sexual assault (rape), is the "ultimate invasion of privacy" and often happens in private or semiprivate places. My assault occurred on the threshold between public and intimate space.

Rape is domestic. The house and the transitory spaces within buildings are regular places of attack but they do not appear to be the responsibility or fall under the jurisdiction of government forces, nor are they the clear responsibility of city departments. There is a building department code that provides strict fire protection, but no crime protection codes exist. The only regulations required by New York City Housing Preservation and Development are limited to doors, windows, locks, and gates, and are badly enforced. Looking at data from the US Bureau of Justice Statistics, I became aware that while serious crimes in general—homicide, robbery, and assault—have decreased, rape and burglary have remained stable for the last fifteen years. Burglary and rape are both crimes that occur in or around the home. The effort to secure buildings, tenants, and the home not only doesn't work practically but also isolates the victim. Energy could be better spent in making the potential intruder feel exposed, rather than safe in the anonymity of transitory spaces. Home is not a safe place. Its familiarity and the routines it produces make women trustful of home, but also easy prey. I was raped in my own apartment, in my own bed.

Despite these statistics and facts, rape remains shrouded in secrecy. The sanctity of the home and the body, and the fear of the ultimate invasion of privacy, is perverted by society distancing itself from the victim. The crime occurred in your home, not mine. Shrouded in secrecy and silence, the victim is implicated as at fault.

Unbeknown to me, my assailant knew my space. He knew the building's security conditions and where to wait for a victim without being seen. The super told me he was staying on the roof of my building, but didn't explain why. He'd attacked me in the early afternoon. Clean and well dressed, he didn't seem to be homeless. He was familiar with the swimming pool and might have showered there. He appeared to be local. I could tell he stayed nearby, as I was raped in the middle of winter and he wasn't wearing a jacket. I'd now encountered him twice, and had wondered why he'd come back to the location of the rape. I realized that he hadn't come back. He never left. The building was his territory.

Detective M was in charge of the investigation. He wasn't helpful and disregarded indications that the rapist lived close to my apartment. He showed no concern for my fear that the rapist would kill me because I reported the assault, and dismissed the possibility he might come back. I was angry that the police did not watch my building, waiting for my assailant to reappear.

In the week following the rape, Detective M arranged for a sketch to be made of the assailant. I met with the artist who was to make the drawing of the rapist at an isolated police building downtown late in the evening. I described the man's features, and the artist tried to represent them. I had my own drawings I'd made of him. Compared to the police artist's my sketches were cartoonlike, vivid but not descriptive. While the artist was sketching he got a phone call and stopped to discuss a grocery list and his children's homework. I was shocked that he'd taken a personal call while I was there, but hearing about his daily routines made me sad. I had no routines anymore. A stranger had broken them. I held back tears. It was difficult to describe someone who, for me, didn't have a face. Or rather, his face was a mask that represented death. While the artist was drawing, he told me the sketch might be posted in the area where the rape occurred.

By the time I gave the OK to one of the drawings, it was 11 p.m. The building was silent and almost empty.

"Who sent you here? You shouldn't have come here alone."

I got up to leave but anxiety about the future overtook me.

"I understand that the purpose of this sketch is so that the police can recognize suspects, but under no circumstance should they post it in the neighborhood until I have moved away completely. He will kill me. Detective M, who sent me here, does not understand that."

"There's nothing I can do about it. I just draw."

He showed me the way to the elevator.

The next day I called the Manhattan Special Victims Squad and requested that they not post the drawings on the street. Panic-stricken, I followed up with a letter. The Special Victims Squad is responsible for investigating all sex crimes and child abuse cases within Manhattan's twenty-two police precincts. While other units are titled by the nature of the crime, the one dedicated to rape is named after the victim, stressing care for the victim rather than law enforcement. I couldn't help but think that displaying the sketch of the rapist on the street wasn't a way to care for my safety, it would only put me at more risk.

In spite of this, the second time I encountered him, the rapist hadn't shown any sign of anger or made a retaliatory gesture. He probably believed I hadn't reported the rape. Or, he'd convinced himself he'd done nothing wrong, or that the rape never happened. If he was aware that I'd reported him, the chances of him attempting to kill me would increase. To calm myself, I tried to see it from his perspective; since there was no visible aggression, he could say the sex was consensual. Perhaps this was a convenient fantasy for him, one that would have been impossible to maintain if there would have been a murder, in which case, the body would have been unquestionable evidence of a crime.

On April 30, 2001, three months after the attack, Detective M signed a follow-up complaint requesting for the case to be marked as closed. Despite this, I periodically called the Special Victims Squad over the next two years, to ask if there was any news for me, but there never was. During one call I learned that Detective M had retired from the Manhattan Special Victims Squad and Detective B had taken over. I thought this would increase the chances of the man who raped me being apprehended. But it didn't. Each time I called I was overcome by the same feeling of hopelessness. I was just another woman raped in a poor neighborhood.

HOW AND WHY I STARTED A LAWSUIT AGAINST MY LANDLORD

ON THE DAY FOLLOWING the attack, I was in the Police Archive on Amsterdam Avenue looking at mug shots, in the hope I might identify the rapist. The process seemed endless and senseless to a degree, because the selection was based on my estimation of the attacker's age. I could remember his features, but wasn't certain of his age. I made an effort to guess, but worried my guess might be wrong. I realized that I could be looking through a vast catalogue of images that might not include my attacker. I asked if we could conduct the search in a more random manner and look at various age ranges, since I was a poor judge of age. But because the police organize the photos in age ranges, I was told I had to review each range in sequence, finishing one before I moved on to the next. My recollection is that the age range I looked at was twenty to twenty-five. Several years later, I learned I had misjudged the age of the man who raped me. He was nineteen.

The session took hours, and while I was there, I anxiously wondered how I could avoid being assaulted a second time.

As I focused on the mug shots, I struggled to contain my fears. I felt trapped in the Police Archive, engaged in an absurd search, and was terrified about the assailant returning to look for me.

Finally I spoke out.

"What if the rapist is not here in the pictures but in my building waiting for me? Am I supposed to go back to an unprotected building?"

"Calm down. He will not go back; they never go back," a male police officer said.

I didn't believe him. A policewoman was staring at me silently, but it seemed to me with empathy. While a new mug shot file was fetched, I called the landlord's office again, and asked for the locks to be fixed. I said I had been raped in the building.

"You might as well be dead," the man on the phone replied.

Later I learned that the office had similarly responded to another tenant, one of my neighbors. She'd asked that the roof doors be locked after she'd been robbed in her apartment.

"Do you think you live on Park Avenue?"

Two men had made their way into her apartment at gunpoint. One of them had pushed her child to the floor. The woman was also violently pushed down, but the father struggled with one of the gunmen. The child saw his father wrestle the gun from the man and pull the trigger, but the gun didn't go off. He watched the other intruder point a gun into his father's face, as he crouched in fear with his mother. The thieves tied his father's legs and wrists with duct tape, and ransacked their home.

I asked the police officers if they could force my landlord to replace the locks and was told they had no authority to change the locks on a privately owned building. They also explained that though they couldn't send a squad car to guard the door of my apartment full-time, they could help me find a shelter.

"I don't want to go to a shelter."

I didn't want to go to a shelter and feel even more displaced. I wanted my home to be safe. Before the assault I had repeatedly asked the superintendent to fix the locks and had complained to the managing office about the lack of security. Nothing had happened, and I was confused about who was responsible. The police told me that the owner was ultimately responsible for the locks in the building, and that he owned not just my apartment, but the entire building. I had not assumed this because it is very rare for one person to own an entire apartment building in Spain, and responsibility for maintenance is normally shared communally. When you live in a dangerous situation in Spain, responsibility is transferred to a Juez de Guardia, a judge who has the power to overrule maintenance agreements and enforce other rules. I couldn't understand why the police wouldn't do anything to enforce security in my building, or who else could.

"Can I have a phone and the Yellow Pages?"

I was embarrassed to make so many requests, but I was desperate. Looking for help to pressure my landlord into securing the building, I randomly called hotlines, lawyers, and tenant organizations. I discovered I could open a procedure in a housing court to secure the building, but that the process would take a long time. I also found out about negligence lawyers, who would pursue compensation for damages. However, they could not enforce security in the building either.

By the end of the first day at the Police Archive, I was exhausted, and I realized I would have to make a lot of changes in my life. Staying in a building without a minimum of security, in which I had already been assaulted, made me vulnerable to another assault. Since my immediate need was to avoid further misfortune, I had to move. I had been forced into accepting the dictum pumped out by my landlord's office: *If you don't like it, move out.*

In the evening, returning to my apartment on the subway, I reflected about how being poor is not only a condition, but also a qualifier. Poor defines a person as less valuable.

It was my need to reclaim my own value that later led me to start a lawsuit against my landlord. I was determined to prove his responsibility for protecting me as a tenant, and to expose his failure in doing so by suing him and requesting compensation for the damage done to my life. The lawsuit and compensation were means to state my value as a person in his language: *money.*

I made an appointment with one of the law firms I'd found in the yellow pages. I met the lawyers, told them what happened, and signed a retainer agreement. Weeks passed and I didn't hear from them. In the meantime, I abandoned my apartment and lived temporarily at my boyfriend's brother's home. Sadness and anxiety overwhelmed me. I read the pamphlet that I was given about the crime crisis program at St. Luke's Hospital. They offered basic resources including counseling, psychiatry, and advocacy. I made an appointment to seek counseling. During a session with D, my social worker, I expressed my frustration about finding another place to live. I also told her I hadn't heard from the law firm I'd contacted. She gave me the names of two lawyers specializing in suing landlords in violent assault cases involving lack of security. I called both. One of them, M, was available right away, and she had sounded very passionate during our phone conversation. In M I found a lawyer who addressed my case with the care it deserved. She believed that lawsuits such as mine were a way of bringing those who don't act on their obligations to justice. Later she told me that she, too, had been sexually assaulted, and was motivated to study law when she was unable to find sympathetic lawyers for a negligence suit.

My life was worth less than the cost of a lock to my landlord. He'd showed no concern for me, and his lack of action was a form of cruelty. Finding the right lawyer didn't solve the problem of the lack of security in my building. Despite my pleading, the lock on the main entrance to my building remained broken, and the roof door unsecured. As a tenant, I couldn't control the security of my building because I couldn't legally change a main entrance lock on the landlord's property. If my landlord did nothing, my hands were tied. There was nothing I could do. I could only complain. I heard from other renters that a common diversionary strategy for negligent landlords was to dismiss a tenant's claims and accuse the tenant of instigating trouble. Instead of listening and fixing problems, negligent landlords react defensively. Perversely, the person experiencing the problem is accused of being a problem. The landlord is, at least rhetorically, released from any obligation to the tenant. But this denial of responsibility is not a valid response: it is an abuse of power.

Whether the lack of action from the landlord was due to apathy, or for reasons related to profit, was not clear. I thought about the "Million Dollar Block" phenomenon, and how the lack of security made the building an easy target for criminals, driving out tenants, thus leaving apartments empty, free to restore, and making them exempt from rent stabilization. In organized crime, conditions in which crime can occur are created. It's rendered invisible, appearing not to exist, much less to be criminal. A landlord's Machiavellian and organized operation, in which violence is permitted but not visibly present, is the business of organized crime. If his inaction was premeditated, and the building was deliberately left unsecured, he was part of corrupt property scandals and his income might be illegal.

When we received our lease papers, the names listed for the landlord were West 129th Street Realty Corp and Green Realty Management Company, both with the same address. This confused me. I didn't know who was the landlord and who was the agent, and which was responsible if we had a problem with my apartment or the building. During the process of the lawsuit, I learned that my landlord had other companies with similar names: West 129th Street Realty Corp d/b/a; Green Realty Management Co. LLC d/b/; and 408–412 West 129th Street Associates LLC. I also noticed that the real estate agency was managed and owned by the landlord at the same address.

As we were about to sign the contract, M, an employee of the landlord, had requested an additional month's rent for what she said was the broker's fee. She didn't want to give us a receipt but finally wrote on a piece of notebook paper: Received $831.00 in cash for 408 W. 129th #29 María Rodriguez. To cover this, we arranged to sell the old car we'd left in Princeton. M had arrived in a new, red convertible sports car. For her fee I gave up the car I had learned to drive in. Later I found out that it is illegal for the landlord to charge a broker's fee if the managing agent and the landlord are the same. However the landlord had collected a broker's fee from my boyfriend and me.

My building, at number 408, and the adjacent building at 412, shared a common exterior wall and roof. They were large buildings; each occupied two standard building lots.

Because of this each street address was doubled, 406–408 and 410–412. My landlord owned both buildings, and both were sites for crime complaints and arrests. There were fewer reports of crimes and arrests in 412, perhaps because W, the superintendent of both buildings, lived there and exercised greater control over the building. My landlord, the superintendent, and their agents knew that the building had trespassers but neither the superintendent nor his agents advised me of this problem when I became a tenant in 2000. During the course of my lawsuit I found out that my landlord had, in fact, signed an affidavit recognizing the presence of individuals trespassing in the building and using drugs in 406–408: "I am the managing agent of the 406–408 West 129th St. The building has many legitimate residents. Recently, trespassers have come to use the building as a place to buy, as well as use, drugs. Accordingly I have asked the 32nd Precinct to arrest anyone found trespassing in the building. I have made it clear that if a person is not a tenant, his presence in the building is unauthorized, and he should be arrested for trespass. The building is posted with signs saying: No trespassing. Tenants and their guests only (07/9/1998)."

My landlord, or someone from his office, filled in a complaint report. The victim's address was the same as my landlord's. Under "Offense(s) if Any" was "BURGLARY 2F," and the date of the occurrence was 04/04/97. Under "Location of Occurrence," the address was 412 West 129th Street. Under "DETAILS" was, "At T/P/O Building manager states unknown person did damage front door hinges to apartment #19 (vacant apt), gained entry, removed 3 doorknobs to 2 bedrooms and 1 closet without permission or authority. Tenants in contiguous apartments, #20 and #21, never heard any disturbance." The report claims that three doorknobs with an estimated value of fifty dollars were lost.

Another police report, also classified under "Offense(s) if Any, BURGLARY 2F" was more alarming. The date of occurrence was 04/02/98. Under "Location of Occurrence," the address was also 412 West 129th Street. Under "DETAILS" was "Compl. states at T/P/O while in her bedroom at above location, she heard someone break the frame of the front door and enter apartment. Compl. states she hid under the bed & heard (3) males roaming around her apartment taking the above listed items. Compl. remembers hearing one perp call out the name of Kevin to the others. No further description."

A few weeks before my scheduled trial, my lawyer located the woman to whom the landlord had replied "Do you think you live on Park Avenue?," and she volunteered to testify about what happened to her family. Under "Offense(s) if Any" was "ROBBERY 1F," the date of the occurrence was 12/01/2000 the time 13:00. Under "Location of Occurrence," the address was 412 West 129th Street. Under "DETAILS" was "At T/P/O Compl. states perp #1 knock on door states had a package from Fed. Express. When Compl open door perp #1 told compl to sign this. That when he displayed gun.

Compl. attempted to close door, perp #1 then pushed way inside apt. perp #2 then entered, compl began to fight with perp #2. This is when perp #2 put shotgun in compl's throat. Perp #1 stated that is not a game will shoot. Compl was then tied down to chair with duct tape. Perps then began to search apt. without permission or authority and removed above listed property."

Another report, under "Offense(s) if Any, ROBERY 1F," date of occurrence 10/16/2000, read: "At T/P/O Building Compl. states while entering his building in the lobby, 3 perps grab him. Perp #1 held a knife to his throat while perp #2 and #3 removed his walkman and his cell phone; then perps fled building."

My lawyer M hired a private detective to investigate the buildings. He compiled a list of actual crimes that were committed, and arrests made by the NYPD in these two buildings between 1988 and 2000. The report referenced twelve burglaries, three robberies, and nine assaults: all violent crimes. He concluded: ". . . There is no doubt that these two buildings are situated in a high crime area and based on the number of reports that I have been able to review and my many conversations with members of the 26 Police Precinct these buildings are vulnerable. I also viewed a countless number of NYPD Reports where arrests were in fact made of perpetrators who reside in either 408 or 412 West 129th Street. So you see not only is the building suspect for crime committed within but there are also known perps to the NYPD that reside within. In addition the Superintendent has given a signed statement as to unknowns stuffing papers in the door jamb at 412 West 129th which in fact renders the door useless for locking/security. Once inside the building and prior to your incident, miscreants had the capability of going from building to building without any problem because the roof doors were always open. BINGO!!!"

In the process of preparing my lawsuit against the landlord, it became clear my assault wasn't an isolated incident. Perhaps the number of crimes in the building was related to a failure to provide security. Following the records of tenant complaints, and building violations for lack of security registered in the City of New York Department of Housing Preservation and Development, it appeared that the landlord had left the building unsecured for years.

"Arrange and make self-closing the doors entrance at 5 sty northwest apt (Date reported: 04/03/1996); Properly repair the broken or defective inoperative intercom system (Date reported: 06/05/2000); Arrange and make self-closing the doors entrance at apt. 8 (Date reported: 07/07/2000); Arrange and make self-closing the doors entrance northeast apt. 2 (Date reported: 07/22/1986); Replace with new the broken or defective door hinges (Date reported: 07/07/2001); Remove obstruction bars and unlawful gates from window to fire escape to provide approved type gate. Rear West apt 6 (Date reported: 10/09/1985); Remove obstruction bars and unlawful gates from window to fire escape to provide approved type gate. Southeast apt. 4 (Date reported: 5/08/1987); Arrange and made self closing doors the doors east and west bulkhead to roof (Date reported: 10/09/1987); Remove the illegal fastening slide bolt capable of padlocking East & West bulkhead door to roof (Date reported: 06/06/1995); Remove the illegal fastening slide bolt capable of padlocking East & West bulkhead door to roof (Date reported: 04/02/1999); Remove illegal fastening lockable slide bolt, at door in entrance located at apt 17 (Date reported: 07/17/2001); Remove illegal fastening double cylinder key operated lock installed (Date reported: 12/28/1989) Violation summery report for the building violations provided by the City of New York Department of Housing Preservation and Development, Division of Code enforcement."

I was concerned about the capriciousness of negligence cases, but knew that it was the only corrective mechanism available. Through coersion, the rapist took control of my body; I was the victim of a crime. Being raped in my apartment, in a building that lacked proper security, I was also victim of the landlord's profiteering, because he'd left me exposed. Rape is a crime and a rapist can be convicted and sentenced for the act. But exposing a tenant to the risk of violence is not considered a crime, and only after a violent crime has occurred can the landlord be held accountable.

The assault had truly damaged me. Every single action in my everyday life was now questioned. Now everything took more than one try. On my way to visit a museum, I would get off the subway and return home without ever reaching my destination. I would arrange meetings with friends and then cancel without explanation. I was constantly doing and undoing, needing to be alone, but unhappy when I was. Less social, I stopped attending reunions and parties. I seemed to have lost the ability to empathize with others but nonetheless I missed meeting new people and exchanging ideas. The belief that my life could randomly be cut short made it hard for me to pursue long-term projects or relationships. I was still disciplined but I didn't have the same enthusiasm. My world had shrunk.

THE CRIMINAL
PROCEDURE AND THE
CIVIL LAWSUIT

HOW THE ASSAILANT WAS CAUGHT

IN THE SUMMER OF 2003 I was in Madrid working on a competition for social housing in Tromso, Norway, when I got a call from M at the New York County district attorney's Office.

"The assailant was involved in a shooting. Remember we found DNA on the cigarettes butts he smoked in your apartment? His DNA matched," M said.

We arranged to meet when I would get back to New York in September. When I arrived in the States I contacted M who told me, "Detective S will be calling you soon to discuss the case."

I didn't know anything about Detective S at that time. Here I'll use a summary of his career made by someone else: ". . . In 1995 he requested a transfer to the Manhattan Special Victims Squad where he began specializing in investigating violent sex crimes. In 2001 he created and initiated a program that allowed him to specialize in and investigate the trickle of incoming DNA based cases that was correctly forecasted to soon turn into an avalanche. As the DNA data-banks began to churn out DNA cases, Detective S and his partner . . . became the first DNA Detectives in the NYPD where they led both New York City and New York State in DNA arrests and indictments while working out of their Manhattan office."

Given my bad experience with detectives thus far, I asked M to meet me before I saw the investigator. I met with M at the district attorney's office. She told me the rapist had been involved in a shooting, arrested, convicted, and sentenced to eight years in prison. M said he'd also raped another woman a few months after my assault. The woman was working as a maid in a hotel at the time. M explained that when a person is arrested for a major crime, the police run a DNA test. His profile matched the profile of the male wanted for two rapes in Harlem. His DNA matched the samples from my rape kit. M handed me her card, *Senior Trial Counsel*.

She added that at the time of the attacks the rapist was homeless, and living on the roof of my apartment. When I heard this I knew my intuition had been correct. He had been capable of using the gun and shooting me. As he was not wearing a jacket in winter time, I had assumed he lived close by. He didn't venture far to commit his crimes. He'd raped me, and the other woman in the area he lived in.

Detective S was in charge of the investigation of the two rapes. The police interview with the suspect, signed by Detective S in 2003, reads:

"Williams stated that he is 25 yrs old with a DOB ——82. He claims that prior to his last arrest in 2002, he was homeless. However, he has family at ————1xxth St ——. In 2001 he was staying in a vacant apt in a building on W1xxth and Morningside Dr. . . . He had an Aunt in that building and she used the apt for storage. Williams was allowed to live in the apt."

This description of the suspect as homeless was consistent with the superintendent's statement on the day of the assault. He'd seen a man matching my description of the assailant apparently living on the roof of the building in which I was raped. However, he did not look like a vagrant. He'd mentioned that his relatives in the neighborhood had an apartment where he could stay. But he wasn't rooted to any place. Unemployed, he lacked a position in the world. Despite his normal appearance, he was living in the interstices of the city, the hidden niches and semipublic spaces of private buildings. He was invisible.

The second rape the suspect was being investigated for took place in a hotel.

"The N.E. Hotel was introduced to the conversation . . . Williams claimed that he never heard of the hotel and had never been there. He denied knowledge of the Hotel several times."

Detective S spoke about the location of the crime without mentioning anything that happened there. The detective didn't ask if he had been there, but the suspect, by denying that he had been inside, anticipated a line of questioning, which implied he knew about something that happened there, inside the hotel.

"The undersigned advised him that it was the hotel on West [. . .] and [. . .] Ave [. . .] At this point Williams mulled over the fact that a street and avenue was used to better describe the hotel." By mentioning the address, Detective S questioned how the suspect, who was living in the area, hadn't noticed the hotel. "He soon declared that he does know the hotel—but only from passing it by on the street as he traversed the neighborhood. He states that he rode his bike past it and knew some people who hung out on the corner from the school [. . .] However Williams continued to claim that he never had been inside that hotel [. . .] The undersigned showed Williams a photo of the hotel's exterior taken from the street by the undersigned. He looked at the photo and declared that he does not recognize it at all."

Apparently in sympathy, Detective S offered an easy way for the suspect to justify not having noticed the hotel.

". . . asked him to look closely and suggested that the green awnings might be new, but the general appearance and the architecture of the exterior façade was certainly unchanged." Now that the architecture and the façade were brought up, "Williams then said that he did recognize the building—but not as a hotel . . . However he did recognize the photo of the hotel as the hotel . . . that he would pass by on his bike . . ."

After I read this interview, I went to the hotel and without thinking, entered. The building had seen better times, but it was still in good shape, especially compared to most of the hotels in the area. Inside it was carpeted and cozy. You wouldn't forget it if you'd been in. I asked for the price of a room. The clerk handed me a card and gave me the rate for two and four hours.

"He insisted that he was not familiar with the hotel and has never been inside it . . . not only did he never stay in that hotel, he has only stayed in one hotel in his entire life. It was a hotel in Atlantic City when he was a kid."

Changing his interrogation tactics, Detective S ". . . confronted Williams with the fact that he had been positively placed inside the hotel . . . Williams continued to deny being inside of the hotel. Williams also claimed to never have used a false name—he has only used his real name and never an alias. Upon further questioning he admitted that he had used an alias in court."

The interrogation method appeared amicable, with the interviewer commenting on subjects, rather than questioning the interviewee directly and without telling the interviewee in advance what he was looking for; it was never implied that the interviewee was, in fact, suspected of committing a crime. This technique built anxiety in the subject of the interrogation, because neutral questions were only meaningful to him if he was guilty.

In the course of the interview, the questions moved on from the location of the crime to the victim.

"The undersigned asked him if he ever met a female Hispanic who worked in the hotel as part of the housekeeping staff. He said that he had not. The undersigned showed Williams a photo of the compl. taken around the time of the attack. Williams saw the photo and stated that he never met her and never knew her. He claimed that he never saw her before. On a copy of the photo he wrote that he 'never see her before' and signed his name underneath."

The questions are asked in a general manner, and when they are denied, specific references of the event are shown. Not all types of reference, only photographs. Nothing is happening in these pictures. They show no evidence of crime, only a building and a woman. They are shown in an attempt to trigger an emotional response.

The interviewee responds "no" the first time the question is asked; after a few inquiries the answer becomes a "yes, but." After each denial, the interviewer presents evidence.

The method builds a case against the suspect, who implicates himself. He starts to anticipate that after each question irrefutable evidence is going to follow.

"The undersigned advised him that he was last seen leaving the hotel by climbing through a window and out onto a fire escape . . . He was told he was seen in the hotel on 2/2/01 and 2/3/01 . . . With the compl's photo still on the table Williams was advised that his fingerprints were found in the hotel. Williams was provided with the Latent Print Unit report which he read. At this point Williams admitted that he had stayed in the hotel—but not as regular as the undersigned claimed. He stated that he was not in the hotel 2/3/01. However he cannot recall when he was there."

Until this point the questions are mostly conversational, but from then onward they imply an answer and become accusatory. Likewise, the suspect's answers are no longer evasive but straight denials.

"Williams was starting to get angry and stated in response to the undersigned's suggestion, that he did not have an argument in that hotel and was never asked to leave the hotel. He claimed that he never had an argument with a hotel maid as the undersigned suggested. He claimed that he never encountered a hotel maid and never encountered the female in the photo."

During this part of the interview the photos related to the crime remained on the table in plain sight.

". . . Williams denied that it was his fingerprint found in the 2nd floor hotel room. He had no explanation as to how the police came up with his prints in that room. He insisted that he was not in the 2nd floor or in that 2nd floor room . . . When asked what occurred in the hotel that day, he said "I don't know." The compl's photo was still on the table . . . Williams continued to insist that he was not in that room. He suggested that perhaps he had touched that bag and had gotten his latent prints on it and that the bag was brought into the room at a later date."

In response to the suspect's attempt to evade the line of

questioning: ". . . at this point the undersigned confronted him with the rape allegation and his DNA was recovered from the compl's panties, from inside her vagina and from inside the condom that was removed from the interior of her vagina at the hospital. In response, Williams replied: 'There is nothing to say. Nothing to lie about. I am going down, shit!' The undersigned again urged him to provide an explanation for his DNA being found inside of the compl. His only response was that there was 'nothing to lie about.' The undersigned advised him of the potential charges he might be facing: Rape 1, Attempted Sodomy 1, Burglary and Assault."

Detective S created a pattern of behavior: he showed a picture, asked neutral questions about it, and then commented that the picture was related to a crime. Eventually Detective S only had to show a picture to get an incriminating response; the suspect voluntarily stepped ahead of his interrogator.

"When shown the crime scene photo of the recovered cigarette butt Williams asked: 'They got my DNA on that too?'"

"Williams never denied any allegation that might have been insinuated from the crime scene photos. However, he was made aware that they were crime photos and that a female was returning home with groceries."

During the rape investigation interrogation, Detective S "asked Williams to show his abdomen. He agreed and lifted his shirt. Williams was observed to have a light pigment (pink) mark on his right abdomen to his navel. The undersigned advised him that one of the compls. described that mark."

There was no doubt that this was the same man. When the rapist had undressed, I had seen a birthmark on the right side of his stomach. In 2008 I met a retired Special Victims detective. When I showed him a mock-up of my book, he realized that in the narrative rape report a birthmark was referenced, but that in the original rape report the box indicating the presence of a birthmark was not checked. He explained to me that when somebody is arrested, and checked for body marks, such as tattoos or birthmarks, the first page of that initial report is cross referenced to see if the suspect has committed prior crimes. The woman who filled in the report failed to ask me if my assailant had any birthmarks or tattoos. A mistake in filling, or not filling, in a box on a form is understandable, such procedures lose their meaning when they become bureaucratic tasks, but if this was a profiling mistake on the first page of my report, and if only the first page was cross-referenced with new arrest reports, the mistake was important. Since age, weight, and height are difficult to judge and are general characteristics, distinctive markings could well be the deciding factor in an identification. In the narrative follow-up I gave to another agent, I made sure it was written down that the assailant had a birthmark on his stomach. There are many black males with brown eyes and black hair who wear jeans, but only one was likely to have a particular birthmark on the right side of his stomach. However, Detective S told me that the omission of the birthmark on the report wasn't significant in my case, because neither the report nor the birthmarks data bank go into detail about the kind of birthmark.

Besides physical marks, the most effective way to identify the perpetrator in a "cold case" is DNA evidence. I called the Manhattan Special Victims Squad for months after my rape to ask if they had found any DNA besides mine, only to learn that the samples weren't yet processed. I understood that most of the "rape kits" or "crime scene samples" only get processed once a suspect has been identified due to the high cost. If someone is arrested for a serious crime, DNA evidence is taken and automatically cross-referenced with the DNA evidence of the perpetrators of unsolved crimes. These two statements made me anxious. The chances of the perpetrator being arrested for my rape, with time passing and his identity unknown, were directly related to him being apprehended for another crime, his DNA tested and cross-referenced with any DNA found on my body or at the crime scene. They would only be able to get a match if my samples had been processed.

Current laws allow DNA sampling of criminals with multiple convictions: not only when they are sent to prison, but also in other situations, which greatly improves the chances that a cold case is linked to a fresh crime. But these laws weren't in effect at the time of my rape. What was significant in relation to my case was a policy change in processing rape kits that were taken at some point in the two years after the rape, due to technology improvements and reduced costs.

My 2001 samples taken as evidence were processed. The DNA matched the results from another woman's rape kit, showing we'd been raped by the same man. I don't know whether the DNA evidence came from my body or from samples taken from the crime scene, or when the samples were processed. I do know they were processed by 2003 and immediately produced results. Following the normal procedure at the time, after the assailant was sent to prison, his DNA was sampled, sent to the DNA data bank to be compared with DNA samples of unsolved crimes. His DNA matched that of the rapist. He was identified.

"DOMESTOPHOBIA" AND PRISONLAND

WHEN I LEARNED THAT the assailant had been convicted and sentenced, my mind went back to when this man was in my apartment. I remembered fast-forwarding, searching for anything that could give me a clue to what he wanted. Bits of data flashed through my mind: one out of ten men in the US is or will be in prison . . . *One out of four black men is or will be in prison* . . . The data I didn't process was: *one out of ten women is raped . . . out of the ten, one out of four is raped in her own home.*

A was teaching a class that he called PrisonLand, about the boom in prison construction and prison architecture. I had also written an essay that I had called "Domestophobia: An Approach to the Deconstruction of the Concept of the Domestic as a Pleasurable Space in the US in the 1970s." Was it a coincidence that in our everyday lives A and I were confronted with issues that we were studying, that our academic research was becoming autobiographical?

My conception of "domestophobia" was rooted in two

ideas: one, that the idea of "home" is a myth, in practice it is more like a prison; two, the house is literally a site for violence against women. After the assault, I made a third connection between "Domestophobia" and PrisonLand.

The home, an emblem of the American dream, is only an image. It is only "home" for those who, instead of questioning the customs, morals, and culture in which they live, accept the myth or dream image of home. The house is the physical manifestation of this dream image. But as with any dream, or idea that takes on form, it cannot be materialized without losing something in the process. The myth of the "home" is kept frozen as a dream image, obscuring the reality of property as a gilded cage for the wealthy or a bare cage for the poor—a trap in either case.

The house as an icon of "home" negatively affects those without one, who find themselves without the stability of a residence while it burdens them with a deep feeling of detachment. The "house-less" are trapped by the idea of "home:" shackled by an ideology that equates them with homelessness, in constant search for a "home of their own" and separate from any community. For those who gather some wealth, when "home" becomes property, the owner acquires the attributes of freedom; the house is the only place to feel free. In the process the home turns into a cage, a physical enclosure, from which they are unable to leave. For them, the main worry has become losing their property, not their freedom.

Awareness of the trap of the home might explain why the suburban single-family house, the established image of the "home" in the United States, is now complemented by the apartment. While both are forms of isolation, the single-family house emphasizes "unity"—of family, class, status, and culture—whereas the apartment emphasizes "retreat." The dream image no longer promotes a family unit under a single roof, but rather, a childless couple secluded from, yet in close proximity to the world. Both images represent freedom through property, but where the single-family house achieves it through autonomy and permanence—no landlord, no lease, no shared walls—the apartment emphasizes a new relationship to production: exchangeability. The apartment is presented as a convenient commodity, a product that is easy to buy and sell, divorced from emotional attachment. The single-family house takes time and effort to maintain and is integrated into a disappearing commuter lifestyle. In a rapidly developing consumer world, its function as a life-developing cell, full of activities, now seems archaic. In contrast the condominium/apartment offers a new sort of retreat. The family has been replaced by the couple; leisure and relaxation, instead of work and family activity, are the focus. Like hotel rooms, the "condo" remains anodyne, a neutral exchangeable unit. These new, nonfamily homeowners are not rooted to a place. Operating in a globalized, transitory world, in which the life/work balance is no longer secured by memory, community, or stability, but by financial investment, condo-dwellers investing, buying, and selling and leaving without a trace, as if they were never there.

In New York, during the real estate boom of the late 1990s many tenants lost their leases as rental space was developed into private condos and former suburbanites moved into the city. This process repeated itself recently, although the sudden collapse of the housing market has halted this trend.

For a house to be a home, it mustn't trap those who live in it. If the house were to provide both freedom and roots then the regulations for constructing and trading real estate would strongly prioritize values like attachment and mobility over profit. The house was a priority product in the economy: for developers, for contractors, and for real estate agents worldwide. On a practical level, if houses were considered real vehicles for dreams they wouldn't be treated as just another commodity to be bought and sold in the so-called "free market."

Taking my thoughts about the sublimation of home, prison, and homelessness further, and looking at the situations in which crime rates decline, and yet the numbers of people in prison increase—even as new prisons are built, the prisons in the US remain almost full to capacity—it might be said that prison picks up the fallout from the new economy and provides a "home" by default. The increase in uprooted tenants—transitory, house-less, and homeless—is directly related to the unsustainable price of property, and the celebration of wealth as the only social value. In an impossible search for "home," community, and security, prison appears as the safest option, and delinquency and crime the necessary down payment.

The consideration of prison as the home by default is not far from an understanding of tourism: not as a safe getaway but as a barely disguised form of imprisonment. The corrupting values of property affect leisure. For the wealthy, tourism provides the same ideological structure as those promoted by property.

A and I were shocked the first time that we saw a recruitment table in the Times Square subway. Two men in army fatigues approached us. "Do you guys want to see the world?" They handed us a postcard of a plane cutting through a deep blue sky that said, *Join the Army, See the World*. A told me he had always wanted to fly after reading *L'Aviateur* by Saint Exupery. The army's slogan targeted those who couldn't afford to take holidays but harbored a desire for adventure.

When I came across the statistic that only one out of seven Americans possesses a passport, I instinctively made an association between the fear and fascination of the unknown with the adoration of the domestic. The inability to travel abroad, to face difference, uneven wealth distribution, and the lack of education, are reshaped into a devotion of "the big home" America.

For those who are young and eager to escape their immediate surroundings, but are unskilled, unemployed, poor, and without their own home, the army offers a low-budget travel opportunity. For the wealthy, tourism offers a getaway, a break from the routine of work. Promoting similar values of freedom and leisure as the property market, paradoxically tourism offers another form of containment. The tourist moves within fixed time/space parameters: from the fixed itineraries and secured environment of airports and stations, to the controlled settings of hotels and resorts. The tourist is secluded from the local realities, often confined to a hotel resort, protected from the local culture and political instability. The resort is replicated around the world, operating as a familiar home away from home, with the architecture of hotels presenting a standardized, branded décor, reducing the foreign to a familiar, almost domestic environment. US military bases repeat this replicable model, using the same architectural design and décor; they are an extension of home.

Prison is the no budget alternative. Similar to the perverse deployment of military service as a form of tourism, prison offers another form of escape. Stretching the argument of a desperate search for home, one could say that prison is the *number one tourist destination* in the US: the final getaway.

A crime committed in another person's house is an attack on property, against what that person owns, but it is also a reminder of what the attacker lacks, home. Psychologically, this relation facilitates crimes against property in the house, such as burglary, or violence against the person in the house, because the crime appears vindicated. To attack another person's house is indirectly to attack the person, their right to privacy. In the extreme, to break into someone's body, to rape, is a means of entering both the home and the body at once. The rapist's desire to feel at home is fulfilled by being in the body of another; and his denial of the need for home is performed through the violation of the other person's body. Whether known to the victim or an unknown intruder, the rapist territorializes the home and the body, occupying both. The fact that the gender of rape victims is predominately female and that, traditionally, the place for women is in the home may relate to the identification of the home with the woman's body.

From conversations with other rape victims, and from my own experience, I came to the conclusion that home is always a point of reference. While 75 percent of rapes happen outside the home, it still acts as a center. With rapes occurring in or near the victim's house, the only "excursion" for the victim is going downstairs to drop a bag in the rubbish bin, or a trip to the supermarket for groceries, or even to the laundry room in the basement. The door is open and a man enters. Or he waits for the doorman to go to the bathroom, enters the building, and waits in the laundry room, or follows a victim, and closes the door behind her when she goes into the building, or simply gets into the elevator with a victim, and presses the stop button. Or it happens when attending an after-school program; at the end of class, the assistant teacher takes the hand of a girl; the girl is too disoriented and intimidated to react; the woman takes the girl to her dormitory and blocks the door. Rape that occurs in or near the house is a form of appropriation, the taking of something that doesn't belong to them, the marking of the person as part of their conquered territory.

There may be a certain relationship between the location of the rape and the level of coercive violence. Less violent or "nonviolent" rape often occurs when the objective for the rapist is "being at home": both sex and self-affirmation are sought. The sex appears consensual, something earned through negotiation or seduction; the rapist seeks approval. Violent rape is a challenge to this idea of home: excitement comes from the violation of norms, and from the other person being reduced to their difference, appearing as an enemy or an inferior. In other words, nonviolent rapes place an emphasis on the search for home, whereas violent rapes emphasize revenge, destroying the body and home of the other.

Rapes outside or apart from the home are perceived as a form of punishment, as if the victim deserved the rape for venturing away from parents, partner, or house. The rapist takes advantage of women's vulnerability: a young woman hitchhikes, the driver demands sexual payment from the woman to whom he has given a ride. A woman meets a man in a club or bar, he appears trustworthy and she leaves with him, only to discover that the pick up was planned, and his friends are waiting for her outside, or in his home. Sometimes the act simply exploits exhaustion: a young runaway, worn out from traveling, sleeps on the couch of a friend-of-a-friend who takes advantage of her, or is accosted in a hostel. At other times, rape is related to moments of weakness, such as crossing a bridge with bags and being offered a hand; a young girl taken by the hand into the hallway of a building; a boy playing at a construction site pulled aside by a worker.

All these scenarios were recounted to me. In all of them the rapist takes revenge for the victim stepping away from the security of their home, for women or children stepping into a foreign territory.

An analysis of rape, based on preventing high-risk situations and staying at home, or the portrayal of the "the high-risk victim of rape" that is fixated on concrete elements frequently involved in rape, such as race, poverty, or marital status, can blind us to the most important factor: the relationship of gender to the home. (There is no distinction of gender when rape involves children, and children are treated as women when they are abused. The Special Victims Squad deals with both women and children who are victims of rape and other sexual abuse). Rape is defined largely by gender, and a more accurate analysis would understand that for women, the home is a high-risk situation.

One out of ten women is raped. The statistic sounds incredibly high. However, the statistical number seems to fall far below the real number. Among the women I know well enough to have shared their experiences with me, half of them said they have been raped. My friend L told me that when she was raped, the thought "here it is" came to her, as if rape is something every woman fears and expects to happen. The probability is that a woman has to assume that if she hasn't already been raped, she very possibly will be in the future. And if she has, she may be raped again. The ghost of rape is attached to being a woman.

Besides gender, there are secondary factors that come into play with rape. A major percentage of rapes are committed by family members in the home, implying that perpetrators are systematic abusers rather than psychopaths, which indicates something is badly amiss within social structures. The fact that rapes relate to poverty, especially the perpetrator's poverty, makes it, to a certain extent, a default effect of capitalist exploitation and not simply the result of mental illness. Recognizing the link between hierarchies in a social structure and rape reveals that not only is society failing to take responsibility for issues such as the safety inside domestic dwellings, but also that we need to rethink social structures, such as the family. Recognizing the economic element in rape implies not only having to try to eradicate poverty, but also having to acknowledge how the prioritizing of wealth affects all social relationships.

If wealth is the primary value, the value of a person is determined by how much that person has. If the poor are considered worthless and valueless, they can be taken easily, as society fails to protect them. As crime is often a form of appropriation, crimes against the poor target their bodies, since they have little other property. As a consequence poor women, as the most impoverished, are the most vulnerable.

When looking at the number of crimes per year in different NYPD precincts in Manhattan in 2007, I started to see a pattern. In Harlem's Thirtieth Precinct, the number of violent robberies (316) exceeded acts of nonviolent larceny (211). In the Upper East Side's Nineteenth precinct, the number of robberies was 206, however, larceny increases nine-fold to 1,643. The number of rapes in the Nineteenth precinct is half that of the Thirtieth precinct.

In Harlem, as in other lower-income level neighborhoods, violent crimes are more prominent. In the Upper East Side, as in other more affluent neighborhoods, nonviolent crimes against property, rather than against people, are more prevalent.

By examining the relation between the frequency of violent crimes against individuals and nonviolent crimes against property, and their location in Manhattan, one can see a clear violent-crime zone and nonviolent-crime zone. The mental boundary that must be crossed to harm a body is mirrored physically by 110th Street at the northern edge of Central Park. This street marks the border between an affluent area and a lower-income level neighborhood. Most crimes involving bodily harm, such as murder, rape, and robbery, occur north of 110th Street, in Harlem. It is not that Harlem suffers more crime than other areas in Manhattan, but that the crimes are more severe. Looking at the NYPD rape reports for the two neighborhoods, it was clear that the chances of being raped are higher in Harlem.

Perhaps a rape in Harlem, in the mind of a rapist, is seen as more "casual" than a rape committed on the Upper East Side, since the residents of Harlem are more used to being victimized, and a violent act is less likely to be reported. Perhaps the police treat rape more lightly in a poor area than in an affluent neighborhood. A rapist might consider the difference between raping a poor and a rich person, in the same way that he may consider stealing a diamond or a stereo. An affluent victim may be a challenge, a way to get the most value from a rape, but it is also a greater transgression. To rape a rich person is certainly more risky to the perpetrator, since not only is the act more likely to be reported, it will probably be investigated more thoroughly. A pattern of control and violence is created dependent on the victim's position and ability to respond to the abuse they receive.

My boyfriend and I decided to live in Harlem rather than Greenpoint, although both neighborhoods had a similar rent range. When we took an apartment in Harlem, we were aware that both culturally and racially we stood out in the neighborhood. This made Harlem more attractive to us than Greenpoint. Reflecting on it now, "difference" could potentially act as a dissuasive element in the eyes of a criminal, because it involves crossing a limit; or it might be a stimulus to a violent crime, since it is easier to envision the "other" as someone "less human."

A little while ago, T, a former detective, sent me a web link, which noted the following statistics:

"The rate of rape/sexual assault per 1,000 persons was significantly greater where the annual family income of victims was less than $25,000, compared to those with incomes greater than $25,000, with the greatest risk occurring in families whose annual income was less than $7,500. This same trend in family income and rate of rape/sexual assault was seen among whites, while blacks had similar rates of rape/sexual assault in the $15,000–24,999 and $7,500–14,999 income groups as they did in the less than $7,500 income group."

Despite bigoted images of white women being raped by black men, rape statistics show that perpetrators tend to victimize members of their own race. The premise that a white woman is more likely to be raped in Harlem, a black neighborhood, is a stereotype. But the premise that any woman is more likely to be raped in Harlem, a poor neighborhood, is based on facts. I am white and I have been raped in Harlem, a black neighborhood, by a black man. This is true and it happened, but it also hides part of the reality. The complete story, the one capturing the full reality, is this: I was poor, which was why I moved to Harlem, a poor neighborhood; I am white, and I was raped in Harlem by a man, poor, homeless, and black.

Looking at the prison population breakdown of the US Bureau of Justice Statistics, in mid-2005, the year that the man who sexually assaulted me was convicted for two rapes, nearly 4.7 percent of black males were in prison or jail, compared to 1 percent of Hispanic males, and 0.7 percent of white males. Studies such as "Incarceration and Employment Inequality among Young Unskilled Men" by Bruce Western from Princeton University, and Becky Pettit from the University of Washington, September 1999, showed that out of the 4.7 percent of incarcerated, the majority were young, black, unskilled, and unemployed. The report could be misread as suggesting that the main element determining who is incarcerated is race. In fact, poverty is a more decisive factor than race: most of those in prison are unskilled and were unemployed before being jailed. The breakdown in the US Bureau of Justice Statistics study suggests a prejudicial hypothesis: immigrants, blacks and Hispanics are more likely to be criminals. But the statistics don't address the connection between crime and poverty. To prevent crime, poverty has to be addressed; addressing poverty means providing education and work and good wages and benefits.

The man who raped me fits into all the categories: he is young, black, unskilled, and unemployed—and now incarcerated, one of the 4.7 percent. That he is a "perfect" statistical match to the crime data is irrelevant, but it troubled me. I hoped that detective work would lead to his arrest, and I was happy and relieved when I learned he was in prison, but I was angry that he fit so neatly into these stereotypes.

If one crosses poverty and gender devaluation, the result

is machismo. "Take me" means make me yours through sexual intercourse. By taking someone by force, rape is not only related to appropriation, but also to the abuse of women as objects. Machismo presents the man as the owner of the woman. If a woman is single, she is perceived as having no owner, and therefore she may as well belong to whoever wants to take her. The devaluation is even more marked if the woman is recently separated from a partner and now alone. In that case, she appears as an abandoned object others may take advantage of. In the same link that the former detective sent me, the relationship between rape and marital status notes, "The rate of rape/sexual assault victimization for females was nine times greater for divorced or separated individuals, and six times greater for never married individuals, than the rate of widowed or married individuals."

When I was raped, my boyfriend wasn't around. He'd gone to Spain. If the rapist knew this, I was easy prey with no man to protect me or to claim me as his property. The rapist reported in an interview that he had a common-law wife. His claim may or may not have been true, but nonetheless, it suggested that the rape occurred not because of sexual hunger (since he had a sexual partner) but because of an impulse to appropriate other women.

CENTURIES OF STRUGGLE for women's liberation, and all the battles in my life for independence, have been diluted. Regardless of theoretical equality, in practice women are disadvantaged. They are considered inferior, less than fully human, degraded by their gender. Additional circumstances may devalue specific women further, "Poor, divorced or separated, urban, 16–24 are at the highest risk for rape." Translate this into the language of the rapist and you get: low-value, used and abandoned by another man, not rooted, independent and insecure, she will, in all likelihood, not report the crime.

HOW THE ASSAILANT WAS CONVICTED FOR TWO RAPES

IN THE AUTUMN OF 2003, I informed M I would probably press charges against the rapist, but didn't know exactly when. I needed to think about it further before proceeding and asked her to let me get back to her in a few months with my decision. She was afraid that if I didn't act right after the arrest, I never would. While I understood her concerns on this front, I didn't want to let the momentum of events result in me acting automatically, following a procedure. The fact that the assailant was in prison, serving an eight-year sentence meant he wasn't an immediate potential danger to other women. He wasn't being held on my account either, so I felt no need to act hastily.

A few months later M wrote, asking when would be a good time to schedule a grand jury presentation of my case. I said my schedule was tight because I was leaving New York in a month and under pressure to finalize my thesis, which gave me no time to schedule anything significant before I left. Her question also assumed I had decided to definitely press charges. She was a professional, and knew the procedure and implications, and I didn't. I needed to understand what I was about to do, and what the implications for my actions were. I would most likely press charges, but wanted to take my time in making an important decision.

I didn't know how the American legal system worked. Did I have a right not to press charges, or an obligation to do so? I wanted a step-by-step description of what would happen if I went ahead. I wanted to know how long my attacker would be in prison, and if the other assaulted woman had already pressed charges. When I was assaulted, I'd had no control over the situation. I wanted to regain my sense of control, and part of that entailed understanding the prosecution process before I went through with it.

Two and a half years had passed between my rape and the capture of the rapist. During that time, the case remained unsolved and the file closed. It was what police call a cold case. In those two and a half years, I had tried to distance myself from the immediacy of the crime, but in reality, it had permeated my everyday life. After losing my home, I had moved between friends and roommates six times. Now, after two years of upheaval, I was able to rent an apartment on my own, although unlike the Harlem apartment, I had done nothing to fix it up. Just as I found the beginnings of a stable base, the ghost of the rape reappeared, and I was concerned that something would displace me again.

While I was glad my attacker was in prison, I was also

concerned that my everyday life was going to be interrupted again. I wasn't looking forward to what I could see ahead of me, facing him again, and revisiting what had happened. I felt anxious, I revisited when he'd entered my apartment two and a half years ago. My instinctive reaction was fear. A fear of death.

It occurred to me that if I pressed charges, the rapist would have my name. He could ask someone to kill me, or wait until he was released so that he could murder me himself. I was frightened of facing the rapist again, and of the consequence of a court case involving him. Rape is not only a crime, it is also a warning: I have raped you, but if you cross me I will kill you. Even if my fears were irrational, they were real to me.

I set myself a date by which to decide whether or not I would press charges. A prosecution had to take place within five years of the rape. Two and a half years had passed and I had two and a half years left, during which I had to finish and defend my PhD dissertation in September 2004 if I was to earn my doctorate. I decided to delay the decision, and use this date as my deadline as to whether or not I would press charges against my assailant.

When I went to the police and reported the rape, I knew that if the suspect was arrested the logical outcome of this action would be to press charges. But pressing charges wasn't just a simple technicality. I went back again and analyzed the circumstances of the assault, then looked ahead and considered the implications of pressing charges. I went to the police and reported the rape because I was scared—he'd committed a crime against me, and I was worried he'd do it again, to me, or someone else—and also because going to the police was the only option. I have no doubt I wanted the assailant to be found, but I wasn't sure I agreed with what would follow on from that. The assumption that if somebody commits a serious crime they have to go to prison is based on the idea that crime is a deviant form of behavior, and criminals should be separated from the rest of society. I understood crime as a process, not an isolated action, or a deviance from correct behavior, but rather the consequence of a system that produces a criminal class, and also benefits from it.

Crime is to procure something illegally, to take advantage of what you can do, rather than what you may do. In practice, and in the name of profit, the capitalist system blurs the distinction between the can and the may, between the ethical and the legal, transforming availability into allowance. The criminal follows the logic of the advantage available to them; their real failure is to be hypercapitalist by offering no resistance to capital's logic.

The criminal system penalizes crime, but the socioeconomic system, with its everyday exaltation of wealth, celebrates similar principles. Wealth is founded in expropriation. Almost anything necessary to sustain life, or that might be taken as a source of pleasure, costs money and often the criterion for choosing any action is financial gain. Crime is the incapacity to resist expectation. But economically, getting away with as much as you can is perceived as the action of a winner, irrespective of what you're getting away with, and of whom you're damaging. The "you can do it!" mantra of individualism, encourages behavior that proves what you are capable of rather than encouraging reflection upon one's actions. The American dream has sacrificed equality and fraternity on the altar of liberty and profit.

It wasn't just this. I was also frustrated by government's and newspapers' ongoing arguments over the leniency of punishment and the need to incarcerate more, and the cost of this to the taxpayer. It completely ignored the fact that victims carry the burden of crime suffered. They not only pay the emotional and physical costs, but they also literally pay the bills.

A short time after being taken to St. Luke's-Roosevelt Hospital by the police, I received a letter from the hospital requesting my insurance information. I was billed for the rape kit, which collected traces from the rape and gathered DNA as evidence. Though I was the victim of a crime, I was still primarily responsible for the cost of the emergency room visit. The New York State Crime Victims Board announced themselves on the pink claim form that came with the bill, as the last source for the costs, "Please keep in mind also that our board is the payer of last resort. Consequently, all existing insurance which the claimant has must be exhausted prior to submission to the board."

The agency would only pay if I had no insurance. I had insurance, but was shocked that I had to pay for the evidence to be collected. It was another form of humiliation. I was angry about it. I thought about all the people without insurance, and the shame of recognizing that having no insurance meant they would have to get charity to pay their bills. I wondered if one day we would be billed for the cost of prosecuting and keeping an attacker in prison.

In response to my claim to the Crime Victims Board, a few weeks after the assault, I got a letter stamped as "Lump Sum Decision." Under the "reason for decision" it read: "Claimant is a female, thirty-five years of age, who was sexually assaulted on January 25, 2001 in Manhattan, New York. Total essential personal property of $30.00." A few weeks later, I got a check for thirty dollars. In their view, the stolen thirty dollars was all the assailant had taken from me.

BETWEEN THE MONTHS that followed my conversation with M and completing my dissertation, I used my work to study my fears. My thesis turned into an analysis of a culture and its paradoxes in light of its inability to directly face the most important fact of human life: its limit.

Going through the open stacks in New York University's Bobst Library, I opened every book related to rape and death, not knowing what exactly I was looking for. Facing the thought of prosecuting the man who had raped me, I consulted criminology and law books, reading up on sentence lengths for rape in different states, which ranged from six years to a maximum of twenty. In certain states, I saw that after increasing the sentence, the number of rapes decreased in the following ten to twenty years. Perhaps a longer sentence acted as a deterrent for rape, causing perpetrators to think twice before committing the crime. But I also noticed that in these same states the number of murders increased. Why did the number of murders increase if the crime in general wasn't increasing? I didn't use these random researches in my dissertation; it didn't constitute academic study. I had no background in law, and I was only looking at the studies that caught my attention and only in this particular library. However, what I read was enough to make me think about the relationship in rape cases between the length of sentencing and for rape followed by murder.

This trend, in which the murder rate increased as the number of rapes declined, may have followed the following logic: that women were raped and murdered. But I had no way of assessing how many of the murder victims were raped. If someone is a victim of more than one crime, US government statistics record only the worst crime.

The thought that a rapist, fearing a long sentence, may decide that the safest way to silence the victim is murder, follows a logic, but it is also insane because it reduces one human being to a mere obstacle and elevates murder to the only means of removing an inconvenience. To kill someone in order to silence them is disproportionate. Murder is the

ultimate crime. The remains of a murder, the body, are cor-
poreal evidence compared to the trace of rape, which may
be invisible. Psychologically, killing someone crosses the
greatest boundary. I wondered if the laws determining the
sentences for rape had any deterrent effect. I tried to think
through the mindset of the man who raped me at different
points in time: before the rape took place, if it was planned.
Then after the rape, both in the succeeding months when he
returned to my old apartment building, and in the years that
followed when he was in prison.

In the Autumn of 2004, a year after the perpetrator was
arrested, I returned to New York to teach. I met with M, the
senior trial counsel. She told me that the other woman who
had been attacked by the man who assaulted me had pressed
rape charges, and that they'd been dismissed. M was thinking of combining her case with mine and bringing both cases
to the grand jury.

The other woman was a Mexican immigrant working as
part of the housekeeping staff in a hotel in Harlem where
she had been raped. Ten years before, when I first went to
London to study English, I worked in a hotel as a maid.
Besides being assaulted by the same man, and despite our
differences, we had something in common: we were both
poor, which is why we were both in Harlem. She was poor
and working class. I was poor but partly by choice, having
been a student and then deciding to only work on projects
that interested me. By American standards my income was

considered below the poverty level and was probably less than what she made in the hotel.

I decided to press charges. On December 21, 2004, M, the senior trial counsel at the district attorney's office, and I entered the criminal courts building at Hogan Street. The grand jury was seated in a semicircle, like spectators in a Roman amphitheatre. Behind them, on a raised dais, sat the judge. I was below, in the arena. I swore to tell the truth, the whole truth, and nothing but the truth. The room filled with jury members, around twenty, who appeared to range in age between thirty and seventy. They would determine if what I was about to say was credible, and thus whether or not to dismiss my charges. Many eyes were looking at me. I heard my words reverberate in the room. The jury looked very serious and sat completely still, until I arrived at the sexual part of my narration. Then the sound of bodies shifting in chairs could be heard in the room. I didn't mention the word rape. I didn't use adjectives. I didn't make pained faces, or rearrange my hair, I didn't accelerate the rhythm of my speech. I talked slowly. I didn't refer to what I felt, I didn't say, "it was horrible," I related only the facts. But sometimes my voice trembled.

"The guy left my body after he had an orgasm."

I hadn't meant to say the word. I should have used the more technical term: ejaculation. But that word didn't come to mind. I was mad at myself. Orgasm implied pleasure and evoked sex, not rape. This was rape. The atmosphere was tense, ceremonial, and cold. Nobody asked anything. Staring at me, they seemed to be in a state of shock. There was no movement from the jurors. The walls of the grand jury room were covered with wood and the floor was cork. The room was a room within a room, and the two doors, one directly behind me, and another to my left, each led into intermediate spaces, before leading into a common hallway. What was said in the grand jury room would stay secret, it would be absorbed.

When I'd finished, the district attorney took me by the shoulders and led me out of the room. Near the exit an old man who worked there offered me tissue. He also had wet eyes. The district attorney and I left the building, hugged each other and wished each other Merry Christmas and a Happy New Year.

AS THE MONTHS PASSED, I got anxious; I still didn't know the decision of the grand jury. I started questioning whether my lack of emotion had had an adverse effect on them, and whether they'd not believed me. The case was accepted and the date of the trial set for April 22, 2005. The assailant pleaded guilty to the two rapes, so there was no need for the trial. I was given the option of sending my statement or reading it in the courtroom. I decided to read it in person.

On May 6, 2005, M and I went to 111 Centre Street. Four years had passed since the assault, two and a half years to find the rapist, a year before I decided to press charges, and several months to indict him. The morning I was to read the statement in the courtroom would be the second time that the perpetrator and I were going to be in the same room. But unlike the day of the rape, we were in a room open to the public, and I could say what I felt and what I thought. I entered at the back of the room, and sat in the second or third row. He entered by the front, on the right, and sat in the first row. He was looking down and I could only see his back. Earlier, the district attorney made sure I wasn't going to shout at him or call him names. She hadn't read the statement I'd written in advance. She sat me at a table in the front of the courtroom. I began to speak, but nobody understood me. M told me to start again, to speak up, and to speak more slowly. I did. The room quieted, and after I finished, there was complete silence:

"In the act of presenting charges, my identity is revealed. I have a name, I am recognized as a subject, a person. This should make my assailant aware that I am a person and of the damage of his violent act upon me. But it also implies that he knows who has presented the charges. I fear I could be attacked again."

INSTEAD OF BLAMING HIM, I calmly analyzed the damage done by his abuse. I explained how my relationship suffered and eventually ended. How for years I felt like a refugee without a home. How I lost self-confidence and hope. How I

was constantly sad and lacked enthusiasm. How I felt uncon-
nected to others and ended up isolating myself. How my
perception of life had changed: I no longer looked forward to
the future, I didn't enjoy my present and often thought about
death. How I continually lived in fear. I wanted the rapist to
listen to the effect of his action upon me, and also I wanted
the judge to understand that the rape had not used an excess
of cruelty and violence. I shared the fears I had for my life,
my concern that other women would be raped, and brought
up my fears about the length of sentences:

"This crime is not a rational thing. I was held in my own
house, forced to be contained, silenced, and raped. He applied
cruelty—threatening death—and humiliation—making me
an object, raped—but no more than was necessary to get
what he wanted, not in excess. It was a violent act, because
rape is a violent act, but he wasn't aggressive. I do not hate
him as a person but I do hate what he did. It is not only
that this is illegal, it is that it is also unfair and wrong. But
still complexity must remain, and the knowledge that each of
us is a person and must be treated as such. Believing in the
force of humanity for changing an individual and a world, I
express my will of the sentence to have no excess and to be
rather short than long."

I UNDERSTOOD the legal system as a way of settling mat-
ters, of drawing a line and moving forward. I faced the risk
that my argument would be misinterpreted as implying I

hadn't been raped. But I didn't want to simplify the issues because I was the victim. I wanted to be as fair as if it hadn't happened to me, not to fall into the temptation of excess, now that I had the opportunity to speak. I did it from fear, but also out of fairness. By requesting that the sentence be short rather than long, I may have risked that my attacker would come after me sooner rather than later, while I was very tired of living in fear. When I left the room, I felt as if I was untouchable.

THE CIVIL LAWSUIT FOR IMPROPER SECURITY

THE CIVIL CASE AGAINST my landlord was initiated in 2001, and lasted until the end of 2006. The procedure, the sequence, and all its phases are still not easy for me to grasp entirely.

The only thing that remains clear to me is that the lawsuit was for negligence.

In response, the defendant claimed that I had let the attacker into my apartment, and that the injury was therefore a result of my own negligence. Their argument was simply that I didn't close the door behind me immediately but first dropped the groceries I'd been carrying and then went back to close the door. My argument was that dropping the bags first or not was irrelevant because pushing the door closed didn't lock it. Coming home with groceries, hands occupied, without seeing anyone following me, the natural thing to do is to put the groceries down, and then close and lock the door, since it wasn't possible to close and lock the door without putting the bags down first. I don't know how the attacker entered the main building but he could have come up through the adjacent building and entered mine from the roof, which also had no lock and no alarm; or he simply was in my building already, having taken advantage of the broken locks on the front door, and was watching for an opportunity from a vantage point at the top of the open stairwell. Either way, the landlord was responsible for security conditions in the building that exposed tenants to attackers.

Until I started this lawsuit I didn't know that the landlord had to provide a self-closing and self-locking door to the apartment as part of his responsibility for all doors to the building. My complaints to his agents had focused on the lack of locks or broken locks on the doors to the roof and the entrance. It was only in the preparation for this court case when I saw the record of tenant complaints and building violations that I realized that landlords were obliged to provide self-closing and self-locking door to apartments as well.

The case was complicated by the fact that the rape occurred a few hours before my building was sold to a new owner. The original landlord owned multiple dwellings throughout New York, Pennsylvania, and Florida. He was described by local newspapers as "a slum landlord." The superintendent who worked for the original owner informed my lawyer that he had warned the landlord of the security problem, especially when drug addicts were seen in and around the building. In addition, several months before my rape, a tenant had been robbed and threatened by two men with weapons and knives. This tenant had also notified the landlord about the dangers of leaving the doors into the building unlocked.

My original landlord, the seller, had let the insurance on the building lapse on the day the building was sold. The new owner, the buyer, had liability insurance that covered the day of the rape, but no liability under common law for the conditions of the property purchased, as he'd not had a chance to fix them. However, the new owner was an attorney who practiced in real estate and wrote the contract of sale. He had been given an engineer's report showing the housing code violations on the building, including problems with unsecured doors. Despite these reports the new owner had agreed to hold the seller blameless for anything that happened in the building on the day of the sale. While the new owner had insisted that the seller repair the boiler violations, he chose not to require that the seller fix the safety violations. While one may have sympathy for the new owner, thinking that the good luck of the old landlord was the bad luck of the new one, a closer reading of the situation suggests bad practice on both parts, and that the transaction was undertaken with the expectation that there would be no claims to answer on the day of the sale.

Once my lawyer learned the sale took place on the day of the rape, she included both old and new landlords in our lawsuit. Since there were strong legal obligations and my injuries were significant, it was important to establish whether the old landlord—the seller of the building—or the new landlord—the purchaser—was responsible. My lawyer's take was clear: the new owner was liable. She explained that the contract, written by the new owner, held him legally responsible to pay for any compensation that the jury would offer.

The court ruled in my favor, finding the landlord negligent in not providing a safe building, and ruling that the attack could not be attributed to any responsibility on my part. However, the trial court judged against my lawyer's argument, and decided that even though the contract stated the new owner was responsible for any injuries in the building sustained on the day of purchase, a jury should decide whether the seller knew of the rape at the time the sale of the building was closed. If the jury found he did know of the rape, and had not told the buyer, he would be held responsible, despite the contract of sale.

My lawyer appealed the judge's order, on the basis that the owner that I dealt with, my original landlord, the seller, was responsible for maintaining a building but the buyer, by contract, was responsible for indemnifying the seller, therefore the buyer would have to pay. Based upon this appeal the courts decided that both landlords could be represented by attorneys and participate in the trial as separate defendants, causing a significant delay in the resolution of the case.

Another important issue for liability was related to "Article 16." My lawyer told me that currently in New York,

in cases where a rape victim sues their landlord for inade-
quate security, and the rapist was caught, juries were required
to apportion responsibility between the landlord and the
rapist, even if the rape victim was not suing the rapist.
She added that jurors were required to answer a question
on the verdict sheet: what is the percentage of fault for the
negligent landlord and what is the percentage given for
the rapist?

Prior to the scheduled trial for the civil suit, my lawyer
conducted a phone interview with the rapist after he was
imprisoned. She explained that she was representing me in
a civil law suit against the landlord for improper security in
the building, and that she wanted to ask him if he was on the
roof of that building.

HW: Wow. So, what if I declined and I didn't want to tell
the truth.

MB: I'm sorry?

HW: I said what if I declined and I didn't want to tell the
truth what if just didn't want nothing to do with it
anymore, at least about this.

MB: Well, you know, that's your right. I'm only asking you
if you could tell the truth. We're not suing you, we're
suing the landlord. I would add that the landlord is,
you know, bringing a claim that it is your responsibility and not the landlord's. But we have no lawsuit
against you.

HW: Wow. I don't know. I don't know. I don't know what to say. I really don't want to participate into this, you know.

MB: Uh huh. Well, could you just tell me whether you had been on the roof?

HW: [laughs] Wow. I don't know if I should do that.

MB: What is—how does it harm you?

HW: Huh?

MB: How does it harm you?

HW: It doesn't but I don't know, want—you know what I mean?—I don't want to get involved in that, and I don't feel I have the right to help anybody out in any situation, you know what I mean?

MB: Uh huh. I'm—really, I'm just—you know, in a way I'm asking you for your help, but I'm asking you if you could just tell what the truth is.

HW: Well, I don't know the truth. I don't know. Cause maybe the em . . . you know these other people that's been writing me?

MB: Well, there are two other law firms . . .

HW: No, but did you have any knowledge of them corresponding with me?

MB: No, I didn't know that.

HW: Yeah, well they have been, too, you know, so, I really don't want to—you know what I mean—put them out there, you know?

MB: What do you mean?

HW: Because maybe they might offer me something, or something, you know? I don't know.

MB: I see.

HW: You know, so I don't want to, you know?

MB: So if they offered you something, you would be willing to tell them what they want to hear?

HW: Not what they want to hear, but I would tell them the truth.

MB: Ah ha.

HW: You know?

MB: We're not allowed to offer you anything . . . That's my license . . .

HW: Me. I, ah, me. I, I mean that, I don't know. I don't know what it is. I don't know. I mean I got a long time to think about all that, so I don't know.

MB: Ah, what do you mean?

HW: Huh?

MB: What do you mean by that?

HW: I'm talking bout my time, I have a long time to go, you know what I mean? So . . .

MB: Right.

HW: I don't know, I don't see no, you know what I mean, in helping anybody out, man, I don't see no, you know, significance of doing that. You know, I think about this time every day, so . . .

MB: So, do you blame Jana?

HW: I never said that.

MB: Ah huh.

HW: I never said that. I never said that at all . . .

HW: Well, I don't know, Miss. I'm sorry, I really don't know.

MB: Well, should I call you back, can I call you back tomorrow and ask you?

HW: Why? What, I make a big difference or something? [laughs]

MB: Yes, it does, it means a, it does make a big difference.

HW: Wow. [laughs] Oh, my goodness. [pause] I mean, I'm not getting recognized for no good Samaritan, or nothing, you know, so I don't see no benefit of this, man, for real. I mean I know it may help you out like this. I wouldn't even say that I owe this to anybody, but, I don't know, I just, I'm not gonna say I don't feel comfortable doing it, but I don't know, I don't know. I don't know . . .

MY LAWYER has subsequently argued, "The apportionment law penalizes rape victims for cooperating with law enforcement to apprehend and convict the rapist . . . By permitting these owners to argue that the criminal is responsible defeats society's interest in requiring the owners to take responsibility for protecting people in their facilities from foreseeable criminal attack. Apportionment also defeats society's interest in seeing that the innocent victim is compensated for injuries because criminals who are prosecuted and put in jail usually do not have the financial resources to pay a victim for their loss. Apportionment leaves the victim without compensation, and shields the owner from the responsibility to provide security." While society has an interest in seeing landlords acting according to the law, and in seeing fair compensation for injuries, it also sees criminals as the only perpetrators of crime. It's easier to accept that the rape only happened because of the decision of the rapist.

This conversation between my lawyer and the assailant exposed the flaws of Article 16. Thanks to Article 16, a rapist is ironically still in a position to exert power over the victim. Out of revenge, or, if the landlord had a corrupt intent, for a small payoff, or even for a reward, an assailant could accept full responsibility for the crime, and relieve the landlord from any financial liability. The victim can be victimized again both by the assailant and by a landlord who didn't protect her in the first place. Article 16 is the potential key to this abuse. The very existence of an article that legally regulates the relations and financial liabilities between the landlord or owner and a rapist gives a clue of how many rapes happen in apartments and inside buildings.

When my lawyer first filed the case I thought that the compensation requested was outrageous, but then I realized that it was more a technicality in the complaint than an actually expected amount. Later I learned that going to trial, and being awarded damages was a technicality as well; being awarded doesn't necessarily mean being paid. The liable party may have no funds, or their assets may be hidden, necessitating a further extended legal battle to actually get the legally attributed compensation.

The evaluation of the damages primarily followed the definition of the injury. Despite my claim for emotional and not for professional loss, several unspoken secondary elements were somehow still taken into consideration: in legal terms a person is what he or she has. My income was low. I had been a student for the previous three years, and I was only working part time. A person is also where and how they live. I lived in Harlem because I could afford it; rents were relatively cheap. If I'd lived on the Upper East Side, in a building with a fancy doorman, the award would probably have been greater. Strangely enough my post-graduate education at prestigious universities wasn't in my favor; it made me appear less sympathetic and in little need of compensation. With two landlords involved, the rapist in prison, and the decision about apportion of liability in the hands of the jury, the outcome appeared unpredictable. With only a few days before the trial date, I realized that the award was going to be lower than I originally thought. There was another element I hadn't considered before. I saw that it was a taboo to put a price on emotional loss. I understood money not as a way to cover the loss, which is impossible, but to overcome the disadvantages of the emotional loss.

It had never crossed my mind that we would not go to trial and accept an out-of-court settlement. I expected that we would win, but at this point, given the complicated situation, I understood a settlement was the safest thing to go for. At the same time, I was frustrated. Settlement was not as satisfactory as winning the trial. It felt like giving up, and accepting an award far from what I originally imagined. In a settlement both parties leave with a resolution that is far from what could possibly be the best for each. But to win one has to gamble. A settlement is tangible and has an end date. While explaining the details of the case my lawyer discussed with me the minimum amount I would accept in a settlement. The civil case was settled out of court, one day before the scheduled trial in November 2006.

FOR SIX YEARS after the rape my life was constricted by a task I had to finish: taking the rapist and the landlord to court. I decided to continue living in New York until the rapist was caught and convicted, and the civil suit was finished. During those six years I put myself on hold, not living up to my full potential. I continued with art and architectural work and even with my writing, but I didn't start long-term projects or establish new relationships. My life wasn't an active one, but one of waiting. Also, pressing charges and opening a claim affected my life, my career, and my emotional state. I focused on issues related to rape, crime prevention, the places where it occurs, and tenant rights. But what devastated my life was the rape rather than the lawsuits. In the days following the civil suit settlement I caught glimpses of the person I used to be. I laughed. I was happy. I had experienced a similar confidence when the rapist was convicted and sentenced.

DEFEATED BY NEW YORK

ONE OF NEW YORK'S "TEN WORST LANDLORDS" FACES FEDERAL CHARGES

IN JANUARY 2007, just a few months after the settlement of my civil lawsuit, my original landlord was brought to justice for using a false social security number on a multimillion dollar loan and failing to pay taxes. In the *New York Post*, he was referred to as "one of the city's worst landlords," and was reported to have spent nearly a month in prison for failing to provide heating and hot water to tenants.

For several months during the trial Steven Green remained newsworthy. Excerpts of testimonials in support of him were published in the *St. Petersburg Times*. Lorraine Bracco, actor and star of the *Sopranos*, wrote, "Your honor, sadly, there are some very bad people in this world, but Steven Green is not one of them. We all make mistakes and he has done his best to rectify his mistakes. Steve Green is a very unique person and is not a person who belongs in prison—he is smart, intuitive, interesting, has always been a pillar of strength, and a person all his friends lean on . . ." Joseph S. Gordon, director of development for the Shield Institute, wrote, " Steve has led several successful and memorable special events over the years. I can speak firsthand about his role as event chair of our organization's first benefit art auction and exhibition last spring. That event netted nearly $150,000 in contributions and sales, and focused attention on the creative gifts of artists with disabilities, whose artwork was the centerpiece of the evening. Steve was the driving force behind the fundraising and publicity, and he played a key role during the event as the evening's principal host."

On February 20, 2007, one day after these testimonials were published, Jeff Testerman, a reporter at the *St. Petersburg Times*, and a constant follower of my landlord's questionable conduct, published an article titled, "Philanthropist . . . and a fraud, a judge will weigh his charity against his crimes." He wrote, "At a 2002 charity gala at New York's Plaza Hotel, Steven Green straightened his tuxedo, smiled and relished the moment. . . . Green started his improbable journey to the Plaza working construction. He clerked at a deli, skipped college and built a real estate empire, building by rundown building. Now at age 37, he oversaw a $65-million real estate portfolio, slept in mansions valued at $5 million and flew to appointments in a pair of Cessna Citation charter jets. But as he was feted at the Plaza, the secrets of another side of Steven Green were starting to spill out. A fire had broken out at Amberwood, a Tampa apartment complex he owned. Hillsborough officials found hundreds of code violations."

A blog dedicated to the radio talk show of Daniel Ruth, a *Tampa Tribune* columnist, ran the following post, "Thanks to the media, this story got local attention and exposed the plight of tenants who were the unfortunate victims of Green's greed. If you listen to Green, it's Hillsborough County's fault for condemning the apartments as code violations accrued again and again. If they didn't inspect, there wouldn't have been any code violations. And his 'I'm a good guy because I give to charity excuse' is insulting. Do we allow bank robbers to get away with the robbery as long as they donate a portion of their crime profits to charity? No, of course not. Green is getting off easy with a 33-month sentence, probation, restitution, and fines. He should be forced to live in the same dump apartments he chose to purchase and rent to others."

I was struck by another *St. Petersburg Times* article written by Jeff Testerman, as early as August 2002, which stated, "Landlord's fire claim looks bogus. The day before Thanksgiving in 1999, a fire damaged several units at Green's Cedar Pointe Apartments. . . . Several weeks later, Green filed an insurance claim saying he had a contracting company's bid for the repair at the run-down complex. . . . Tampa Bay Contracting's bid was signed by a dead man." And in May of 2002, Rochelle Renford of weeklyplanet.com wrote, "Transplanted New York landlord Green again attracts law enforcement attention for neglecting his rental units, this time in Tampa. . . . In New York, Green amassed

$3 million in building code fines, owed thousands of dollars to the electric company and was facing lawsuit from tenants . . . since then, Green may have moved from callous to criminal." On another website I read an electrician's description of work he had done for my landlord, "Our boss instructed us to basically cheat to pass inspection. He showed us how he rigged the outlet . . . 'You take a piece of wire, you screw it into the neutral and you screw it into the ground,' . . . and you've instantly got two orange lights, when in fact there is no ground wire at all."

I WAS ONE OF THE FORMER TENANTS who, after learning that my landlord was being brought to justice, sent the authorities my experience in the form of a victim's statements. In a letter, I summarized the circumstances of the rape in my apartment when I was a tenant in one of his buildings in Harlem, New York. I also related in detail all the facts involving my stay in the building, including the signing of the agreement, the confusion over the landlord and the agent, being charged a brokerage fee by the owner, the lack of hot water and heating, the defective gates that had prevented me from escaping, and the broken and missing locks. I sent the letter to T, who was the probation officer on the case, and the person who handled victim impact issues at sentencing.

My landlord's trial took place in February 2007. He was

sentenced to thirty-three months in federal prison for tax evasion and real estate fraud. In May 2007, less than eight weeks before the start of his prison term, he was the subject of a hit-and-run at around 4 a.m. as he was walking to his Rolls Royce near Times Square. More than two years later he began his sentence, but was released after serving less than a quarter of the time due to his "deteriorating health."

DEFEATED BY NEW YORK, OR, WHY I CAME TO NEW YORK

I GREW UP WATCHING American movies in Spain. Until I was thirteen my country was ruled by the fascist dictator General Franco. What I saw of other countries was limited by censorship. Movies on TV were either Spanish comedies, or American movies. The Spanish films—low-budget and mundane—vaguely reinforced family life, financial austerity, and the fascist regime. American movies, in contrast, were Westerns or lavish, spectacular melodramas. I remember the MGM lion growling at the beginning of Hollywood movies, and how I was aware of the ferocity underlying the good life. When I was a child, I thought the Westerns were history, and the personal dramas and comedies—in which the characters were usually rich and beautiful—were plays, unreal fictions. Most of the scenes seemed to take place at night. I remember silver party dresses shimmering in candlelight. Many of these movies were set in New York, but an illusory, painted New York, seen through a window and recorded in a film studio in Hollywood.

My uncle used to hide his copy of *El Capital* among his electrical equipment. Communist books were forbidden, and I grew up seeing the United States of America as the enemy, partly based on the presence of its military bases in Franco's Spain. "Yankees go home!" was the common, if unspoken, sentiment. I didn't associate the America in the films with this United States. But I found myself drawn to both. I wanted to visit the America of the movies, and to understand the USA because it ruled the world. I was fascinated by its wildness and ferocity, and I wanted to go there, to study it up close, and to observe its behavior in order to defeat it.

I didn't go directly to New York when I moved to America. I moved in stages that were like the zigzag mountain paths that facilitate a climb. New York seemed overwhelming, bright, fascinating, but also unapproachable. First I went to San Francisco, a calmer city, to prepare for three months for the ESL English exam. As planned, I stopped in New York on the way back to Spain from San Francisco, and my sister joined me for what was also her first time in the city. I wanted to see the hyper-real deer and monkeys in the Museum of Natural History and meet Duane Michaels, a storyteller-photographer. A had told me to visit the spiral gallery ramp in the Guggenheim, to look at the way the city enters through the windows of the Whitney, and the buildings that look like a stage backdrop from the MoMA garden.

My sister and I arrived after Christmas, and on New Years Eve we skipped Times Square and started 1996 early in the morning by walking over the Williamsburg Bridge. We crossed a deserted and white city and I was so fascinated by the overlap of building types, the different neighborhoods, the signs of ethnic plurality, that I forgot about capitalism. On Mercer Street in SoHo, we visited a friend of a friend who was a painter. The cold city and rat-infested streets disappeared as we entered the unexpectedly warm interior of a luxurious loft. The contrast was like nothing I had experienced before. The building was without transit areas: there were no communal spaces, no possibility of talking to your neighbors in a hallway, and the elevators opened directly into the apartment. The boundary between private and public space was the street. The painter told us it was once an industrial building, before being transformed into lofts by artists who used them as both work and living space. SoHo was a dangerous area when artists first started moving there. Artists put up with the harsh conditions because they found cheap spaces to live and do their work, but the city was then too dangerous to attract many tourists, and they rarely strayed from the attractions. Crime was the city's stigma.

Real estate speculation has followed artists for decades, across New York, in SoHo, Chelsea, Williamsburg, and in other cities, like Berlin and London. After artists move to a place and add value to it, fixing up spaces, setting up small communities, real estate developers and agents arrive, increasing the rent and displacing the artists. On the border of Chinatown, where I have lived since 2003, that strategy has been inverted. Real estate agents arrive first, buying shops and renting them only to art businesses or galleries, as a way of attracting wealthy tenants.

Now, in 2008, the city appears safe, tourism flourishes, but it is filled with dead art.

New York has now become the number one tourist destination, and safety and affordability are inextricably linked. According to a 2008 *New York Sun* article, "a record-breaking 46 million tourists are estimated to have flocked to New York last year, pumping a projected $28 billion into the local economy. . . . Visitors from abroad jumped by nearly 20 percent in 2007, with an estimated 8.5 million tourists hailing from foreign countries." The article goes on to discuss Mayor Bloomberg's radio address the day before, in which he asserted that tourism dollars impact the city's entire economy, adding that crime rates in "the nation's safest big city" will promote tourism for years.

When I hear that crime is going down in New York City I ask myself: What kinds of crime? Against whom? And where does crime move to? Do the crime statistics cover the whole city and all crimes, or are they published to reassure tourists, based on street and personal crimes in "civic areas"? The first time I visited New York I went as a tourist, and I didn't cross the northern boundary of Central Park. Many of the tourist maps finished at the green line of Central Park. Some had arrows that indicate what was missing: Harlem and the Bronx.

In 2007, I googled the addresses of my old apartment and the Clinton Correctional Facility in Dannemora, New York, where the rapist is in prison, and I realized that on two different scales—that of the city and the state—the north correlates with crime, poverty, and incarceration. The highest crime area in Manhattan is located to the north of Central Park, on the northern shores of the island. The Clinton Correctional Facility is located in an area called the "Blue line," which, despite being National Forest Preserves, is an area highly populated with prisons and military headquarters, located in the northern section of the State of New York, right below the border with Canada. In the Western world, the south is usually thought of as the region of poverty, and the north of prosperity. In Manhattan and New York State the geographic convention is reversed, and the north is the home of crime and poverty.

The sweeping of crime to the northern borders of the city and state doesn't entirely displace it. It also creates the conditions for property speculators to target specific blocks in order to create the illusion of safe pockets of housing for affluent residents from the suburbs. Crime is used as one of the tools to socially cleanse blocks—long-term tenants are forced out as a result of deteriorating conditions: landlord malpractice, cheap profit, heavy demolition. New buildings are the result. But the new condo blocks don't create a renewed civic sense; rather than building solid relations they continue the process of the disintegration of communities. But they play a part in the transformed image of New York as a safe city attracting tourists and short-term visitors. When a city is developed to maximize profit from its square footage, and its main industries are entertainment and services, it's hostage to the whims of fashion. It will eventually lose its attraction and start to decay. Even if the city survives economically, the system it relies on is predatory, and the predators move on, from city to city.

During my first stay in New York in 1996, my sister and I sublet an apartment in the Village. We spent our time trying to avoid being tourists. During the day we visited cultural spots, in the evenings we saw friends of friends. We spent our nights recovering for the next day, thinking that here the impossible happens—good or bad—and this was the essence of New York. We lived in New York as many New Yorkers do, as New Yorkers on their time off. We were in a limbo, acting as if we lived in Manhattan but in fact we were detached from the reality of the city.

This limbo, I realized later, was a common way of experiencing New York. Manhattan is not only an island but also a floating city. The population turnover is huge. People come and go in masses, in the city and into the city, from other states and other countries. They come for a day, or for a short-term stay: a week, a year, an internship, a master's degree or a conference. Whether they visit to study or to do business, their frame is narrow: the city is filled with excitement and lots to see, but most people have no time to get involved with real life. Many people move to the city to find better opportunities: part of a domestic or international migration from the countryside or small town to the city.

More people than ever before live in cities rather than in the countryside. In addition the movement of people as tourists or visitors between cities is greater than ever. And cities are now increasingly less civic. Tourists spend money and consume the city, taking whatever it has to offer. Visitors enrich the city but the excitement and their short-term stays prevent them from creating anything new. Immigrants, trying to survive and earn a living, take time to settle and make an impact. Often it takes a decade or even into second generation before they can effect a change. And the city only benefits economically from the flow of people. Excluding them from the central structures of the city, it allows transient populations to change the appearance and the economy of the city, but not to improve or bring about civic progress.

During my time at Princeton I visited the city as another kind of guest. For three years I commuted with A via the New Jersey Transit, to New York on Saturday mornings, taking the train back at night after exploring the city, particularly for professional art opportunities. We went to the MoMA Archive, the Whitney, PS1, the art galleries in Chelsea, the Dia Center for the Arts, and even had a show ourselves in Chelsea.

Sometimes A and I visited his brother at work at a midtown bank. His view of New York was very different from ours. One winter, A and I sublet an apartment on Wall Street, where high-rise buildings populate the skyline. On the street, the buildings act as visual devices, framing the sky into geometrical forms, but the view from the windows was just a wall; one felt trapped in an interior. When coming to the city to visit T, an architect friend from Spain undergoing cancer treatment, we met L. After T died, we continued to see L and spent some weekends with her in her apartment on the Upper West Side. We went to her dinner parties and met her friends. The scene reminded me of Woody Allen movies.

That was the last time I lived the myth of New York as it appeared to me in the movies. New York operates under a double order, but unlike other cities with legally sanctioned commerce and a black market, each having clear rules that run on parallel tracks without crossing over, in New York these two structures—parasite and host—are intertwined, one living inside the other. One structure is easily apparent, but the other isn't, and by the time you see it, it is too late, you are already victimized by it. You only see the trap after you've fallen in.

I fell into the trap, into the world where the rules were unclear to me and the route out was obscure. It took me years to disentangle myself from it. I moved six times, to different neighborhoods, my life designed to always be ready to move. Meanwhile, I worked as a professor for seven years.

Most recently, I spent my days living in Chinatown, writing, doing research, and analyzing New York, and occasionally having worthwhile discussions about it with friends. Now I don't see the city as a place of professional opportunities. The importance of New York is beyond academia, architecture, business, art, or any other field. It is the unexpected reactions from strangers and the occasional encounters that create close relationships that make the city significant. It is not the events but the people that still make New York interesting for me. I circulate with individuals driven by needs that are not easy to meet. Brought together out of necessity, I have discovered a community that transcends mere need. These people, in this New York, create a system of chance in which one finds what one needs when looking for something else.

I cannot see the city that I saw when I first came. From the top of the Empire State Building, New York appears seductively manageable, like a toy city. But at ground level the reality is different. With its bright lights and grand scale, it embodies urban fascination. But as with any seduction, it can only be enjoyed by being apart. This is why New York is the city, the one that one has to visit. Not because it has better attractions than other cities, but because its attraction has to be experienced at a distance.

A liked Times Square more than anything else in New York. I remember being half asleep in the Lincoln Tunnel as I moved to New York for the first time. A driving a rental van as we arrived from New Jersey after picking up our belongings from the house in Princeton, on our way to our new apartment in Harlem. The lights intense. Colored lights, blinding.

—*Mira janopterillo, mira, despierta mira las luces.*

There was nobody on the street. Covered with billboards, the buildings appeared unreal, as if they had nothing behind their facades.

AFTERWORD

RAPE NEW YORK describes my experience of being held and raped in my apartment, then chronicles the events of the following six years. Through my comments on these facts, *Rape New York* examines and reflects on what I consider to be a culture of predation and its crux, the city of New York.

Immediately after the rape, I took a picture of the wrinkled sheets on which I was assaulted. I collected traces of the attack: a plastic cup, cigarette butts. The next day I photographed myself in the bathroom mirror, capturing the estrangement in my face. I also photographed the building in which I was raped. In the years that followed I collected information from the investigations and archived data relating to the rape.

While I was being held hostage and raped in my own apartment, I registered every detail of the rapist's physiognomy. In the weeks following the attack, afraid the assailant would return, I minutely dissected those two hours, analyzing his every word, movement and the changes in his tone of voice in an effort to imagine and anticipate his actions both to protect myself and to aid in his apprehension. Over the years, I continued to analyze those two hours. I brought a disciplinary model of criminology to these details examining incentives, motives, and statistics, studying the rapist's behavior in light of psychological patterns, uncovering a persistent pattern and relationship between the geography of crime and sexual violence, racial and economic exclusion, and unregulated property development.

The rape occurred on January 25, 2001, at 408 West 129th Street, #29, in Harlem. The legal procedures that followed ended in 2007. Both the assailant and the landlord of my apartment have been convicted; the former for rape, the latter for fraud.

ACKNOWLEDGMENTS

I'D LIKE TO THANK Rajneesh Jhawar, who, without meeting, made a generous contribution toward the cost of preliminary edits on this text. I am grateful to many friends for their collaborations as readers and editors: to Adeola Enigbokan for her enthusiastic exchange of ideas, to Gearoid Dolan for his unwavering support, to Gabriel Park for his suggestions, to Keith McDermott for his commitment to working on the text. Special thanks to Simon Lund, who, despite his discomfort with the event that led me to write this book, gave me his help.

Thanks to Book Works for publishing the book first, and special ackowledgments to Jane Rolo for understanding my voice, and to Gavin Everall for his editorial work, which gave the book fluidity and sharpness. I am grateful to Amy Scholder and the Feminist Press for taking a risk and publishing this book in the US.

I would like to use this occasion to acknowledge people who provided understanding and support after the rape and in the years that followed. Daniel Borrego Cubero opened his home to me immediately after my attack. Celina Alvarado and Petros Babasikas are two good friends who helped me move. Leslie Blumberg housed me for months and her friendship was invaluable. My sister, Isabel Leo, was always available in times of crisis and doubt. Angel Borrego Cubero guided me with his clear thinking immediately after the rape as he has continued to do over the years with his friendship. I would also like to thank the professionals who have helped me. Danette Wilson Gonzalez, my therapist, gave me the long-term emotional and practical support. Without my lawyer, Madeline Lee Bryer, my encounter with the legal system would have been nothing more than a second traumatic experience. And finally, Detective Alan Sandomir, Special Victims Squad, and Martha Bashford, Senior Trial Counsel, New York County, District Attorney's Office, without whom my assailant would not have been convicted.